THE WORD
IN AND OUT OF SEASON

Homilies for the Sundays of Ordinary Time, Cycle C

by Richard Viladesau

Paulist Press
New York and Mahwah

also by Richard Viladesau
published by Paulist Press
ANSWERING FOR FAITH
THE REASON FOR OUR HOPE
THE WORD IN AND OUT OF SEASON, CYCLE B

Copyright © 1991
by Richard Viladesau

Library of Congress Cataloging-in-Publication Data

Viladesau, Richard.
    Homilies for the Sundays of ordinary time, cycle C / by Richard
Viladesau.
        p.   cm. — (The Word in and out of season : v. 3)
    Includes bibliographical references.
    ISBN 0-8091-3224-9
    1. Catholic Church—Sermons.   2. Church year sermons.   I. Title.
II. Series: Viladesau, Richard. Word in and out of season : v. 3.
BX1756.V63W67   vol. 3
252'.6—dc20   90-46536
                                                              CIP

Published by Paulist Press
997 Macarthur Boulevard
Mahwah, New Jersey 07430

Printed and bound in the
United States of America

Table of Contents

To my brothers and sisters and nieces and nephews:
to the memory of Ronald;
to Raymond and Jennifer;
to Cathy and Mike, Michael John, Lisa, and Matthew;
to Linda and Dan, Marie, Anna, and Andrew;
to Donna and Steve, Martina, Anne Renee, Stefani and Thomas;
to Mary Anne and Rich and Michele;
and to Christine.

Introduction

In the last months of his life, the great author Leo Tolstoi came to a personal crisis which had been building for many years. Shortly before he ran away from his home and family and died in a provincial railroad station, Tolstoi had written in a letter to a peasant:

> You ask whether I like the life I am now leading. No, I do not. I do not like it because I am living with my family in luxury, while around me there is poverty and need, and I can neither extricate myself from the luxury nor remedy the poverty and need. This I do not like. But what I do like about my life is that I do what is within my power, and to the extent of my power, to follow Christ's precept and love God and my neighbor. To love God means to love the perfection of good and to draw as close as you can to it. To love your neighbor means to love all men equally as your brothers and sisters. It is to this, and this alone, that I aspire. And since I am approaching it little by little, though imperfectly, I do not despair but rejoice.
>
> You ask too whether I rejoice, and if so over what— what joy I expect. I rejoice that I can fulfill to the extent of my powers the lesson given me by the Master: to work for the establishment of that Kingdom of God toward which we all strive.[1]

The anguish Tolstoi experienced in his personal situation—being chained by family and circumstance to a life of comparative comfort, while seeing around himself abject poverty—might easily find an echo in the consciences of Christians in the contemporary "first world." As a society, we

1

enjoy a disproportionate amount of the world's products and use the major portion of its energy and resources. We live in comparative comfort and security, and we take for granted a standard of living and enjoyment unprecedented in history. At the same time, we are surrounded by the almost unbelievable conditions of misery of a vast portion of the human race: the "third world." And, like Tolstoi, we find ourselves unable either to eliminate the poverty and misery or to escape from our own complacent comfort.

It is notable, moreover, that Tolstoi saw not only the poverty, but also the luxury as a problem; if poverty dehumanizes, so does excessive comfort. As Tolstoi saw, the life of luxury is spiritually deadening for two interconnected reasons: first, the well-being of the few is—at least in part—*dependent upon* the exploitation of the misery of the many; second, material satisfactions and attractions can close our hearts to the true values of life and its ultimate meaning: the "Kingdom of God," the value of persons and of love.

Thus, we, contemporary Christians, like Tolstoi, must feel somewhat uncomfortable with our situation; if we have an awakened mind and conscience, we cannot totally like our lives. But, again like Tolstoi, we find there is something that we can like: the fact that we can do something about our condition, that we can strive to follow Christ's commandment to love God and our neighbor.

It follows that Christian preaching in our society must have an essential concern with "liberation." Although the term "theology of liberation" has primarily been associated with currents of contemporary thought in the third world, particularly in Latin America,[2] a reflection on our situation shows that it is by no means out of place in the prosperous "first world" as well.

Indeed, liberation is one way of stating the essential meaning of the Christian message, the "good news" itself. In

Luke's gospel in particular, the work of Christ is seen as the power of God's Spirit bringing the freedom of the kingdom to the alienated world. In the "program discourse" (Lk 4:14–21—third Sunday of the year), Jesus announces that the prophecy of Isaiah has been fulfilled in his person:

> The spirit of the Lord is upon me;
>   therefore he has anointed me.
> He has sent me to bring glad tidings to the poor,
>   to proclaim liberty to captives,
> Recovery of sight to the blind,
>   and release to prisoners,
> To announce a year of favor from the Lord.

The entire rest of the gospel may be seen as the further proclamation and performance of liberation: from physical poverty, hunger, and sorrow (Lk 6:20–26—sixth Sunday); from hatred and mental narrowness (Lk 6:27–38—seventh Sunday; Lk 10:25–37—fifteenth Sunday); from sickness (Lk 7:1–10—ninth Sunday; Lk 17:11–19—twenty-eighth Sunday); from death (Lk 7:11–17—tenth Sunday; Lk 20:27–38—thirty-second Sunday); from sin (Lk 7:36–50—eleventh Sunday; Lk 15:1–32—twenty-fourth Sunday; Lk 19:1–10—thirty-first Sunday); from egotism (Lk 9:18–24—twelfth Sunday; Lk 18:9–14—thirtieth Sunday); from the power of evil (Lk 10:17–20—fourteenth Sunday); from greed and material concerns (Lk 12:13–21—eighteenth Sunday; Lk 12:32–34—nineteenth Sunday; Lk 16:19–31—twenty-sixth Sunday).

As this list alone makes clear, there are many levels to liberation. Its goal is the attainment of freedom: the ability to be or to act, to determine one's existence toward the good. Human freedom, however, is always to be attained by the overcoming of the existential obstacles to such self-determination; and these obstacles are of different kinds.

On a physical level, there is a lack of freedom which consists in subservience to alien forces: the impersonal forces of uncontrolled nature, manifested in accident and sickness (conceived in the ancient world as the reign of personal demonic powers); or the impersonal and depersonalizing forces of economic and social servitude, poverty, and injustice. Obviously, this form of lack of freedom is most significant in those areas of the world which are materially underdeveloped and are dominated by internal and external forms of exploitation.

There are, however, other levels of freedom to be attained even when physical, material, and political liberty are taken for granted. On a psychological level, freedom is the ability to act without compulsion or obsession—freedom from anxiety, from psychic "blind spots" that prevent us from facing reality,[3] from the fear of self-knowledge. While mental health is to a large extent conditioned by physiological and chemical factors, a dimension of meaning is also present. To be free psychologically means also to have the liberty to hope, to find life meaningful, to face the truth about one's self and the world, to be able to apprehend and be attracted by the beautiful, to be capable of giving and receiving love.

On an intellectual level, freedom means the overthrow of prejudice and bias, the courageous opening of the mind, the surmounting of mythology, the ability to attend to the data, to imagine new possibilities, to reach insight, to achieve and to criticize formulations and concepts, to weigh evidence dispassionately, to make sound judgments. It means liberation from inattentiveness, stupidity, and rashness; overcoming the power of obscurantism, the myth of materialism, the narrowness of ideology and unexamined presuppositions.

On a moral level, freedom is the ability to orient one's existence on the basis of values: the beautiful and the good. It implies liberation from slavery to the unintegrated drives of the lower levels of our animal being, to societal conditioning and, above all, to the spontaneous egotism that marks our being as "fallen."

Finally, there is the "freedom of the children of God": the liberation which comes from the acceptance of God's gift of himself; liberation from death and sin; from the constraints of the Law; from the intrinsic limitations of our finitude; freedom for life in the Spirit, for absolute love. This is what St. Augustine referred to as the freeing of freedom itself: the love of God grounds every other dimension of freedom and integrates the whole of human transcendence into a final meaning and goal.

The attainment of any level of freedom implies a "conversion": a transformation of the subject and his or her world.[4] Each level of conversion implies and calls for every other. Furthermore, the attainment of internal or spiritual freedom is intrinsically connected with the achievement of political and social freedom, for it is only by an act of self-transcendence that we can overcome the prevailing "group bias" that prevents us from seeing that the interests of our particular class, group, or society are achieved at the expense of the good of others.[5]

Hence—to return to Tolstoi's insight—the spiritual freeing of the "haves" in our society is inextricably connected with the political, social, and economic liberation of the "have nots," both among us and in the exploited underdeveloped nations of the world. Moreover, without a basis in personal conversion the preaching of the "social" dimension of the gospel will almost invariably be seen as an unwarranted interference of religion—conceived as a purely internal and "otherworldly" phenomenon—with the unspiritual realm of the world, and will meet with resistance and resentment. The preaching of social justice must be able to make a connection between the spiritual—the realm of transcendence—and the concrete circumstances of our daily existence, including our sociopolitical and global situation.

The achievement of this task implies yet another form of liberation which is crucial to the preacher: the liberation of the imagination. Every person lives and thinks within a context, a mental "horizon," which at the same time gives meaning to our thoughts and actions and limits their possibilities. The meaning of conversion is the opening of our horizons (at the various levels of our being) to what is "other" or "beyond": to the transcendent and mysterious, that which is not within our control, but challenges us and draws us out of ourselves.[6] The "other" is to be encountered in every human person, as well as in the Absolute Otherness of God. But the encounter is possible only on the condition that we allow the other to be itself, rather than reducing it to a function of our consciousness and world.

The imagination is critical in enabling this encounter to take place. Through it, what initially is simply "other" can be seen to be in some manner analogous to what one has already experienced, and hence the encounter is revealed as genuinely possible: the unknown, the other, is not merely alien, but corresponds to an openness in one's own being. Our true identity is not locked within our present selfhood or horizon, but is to be found precisely in the dialogue with the other.

It is the function of the preacher to enable the imagination to function on this level of analogy and empathy. This will mean liberating the imagination from its usual and familiar courses, breaking it free of its "common sense," attracting it to a different vision. The means of doing this are multiple. Jesus uses parables to allow the breakthrough of an analogy to our situation. The contemporary preacher may, through a careful exegesis and explanation of the scriptures, attempt to draw the hearer's imagination into an unfamiliar view of the world which challenges our presuppositions, and hence into an insight into the moral challenge of our contemporary world. If the ancient world can be seen as revealing genuine possibilities of the human for us, then the "others" of the contemporary situation may be seen likewise as inviting us to a reevaluation of our lives. (Such a method is particularly inviting in the light of the themes of Luke's gospel, in which Jesus' compassion for the poor and oppressed plays so large and clear a part.) Or the preacher may adopt a more explicitly "correlational" strategy, appealing to the hearers' experience, and attempting to raise from it the question about human existence to which the gospel message of love presents the answer.[7]

It is the latter method which is attempted in the homilies of this volume. The theme of "liberation"—in the social and political sense—may not always be apparent. But every genuine preaching of the gospel will involve an invitation and a challenge to self-transcendence in the love of neighbor; and such love can only be realized in concern for the concrete circumstances of human existence, universally and on every level. It is therefore my hope that these reflections may serve to reinforce that continual call to conversion and liberation in which we are confronted with the Other who is at the same time the deepest dimension of our very selfhood; and that this encounter may bear fruit in a heightened consciousness of our unity with all the human family, and in finding our joy in the resolve "to work for the establishment of that Kingdom of God toward which we all strive."

NOTES

[1] Quoted in Valentin Bulgakov: *The Last Year of Leo Tolstoi.* Translated by Ann Dunnigan. New York: The Dial Press, 1971.

[2] For an overview of the meaning and development of liberation theology, see Hennelly, Alfred T., S.J. (ed.): *Liberation Theology: A Documentary History* (Maryknoll, New York: Orbis Books, 1990).

[3] For an analysis of "scotosis," or the bias that affects the subject on the level of the psyche, see Lonergan, Bernard: *Insight* (New York: Philosophical Library, 1957), pp. 191–206.

[4] Lonergan, Bernard: *Method in Theology* (New York: Herder and Herder, 1972), p. 130. For Lonergan's analysis of intellectual, moral, and religious conversion, see pp. 237–244.

[5] On the "group bias," see Lonergan, *Insight*, pp. 222–225.

[6] For the notion of conversion as a shift of horizon, see Lonergan, *Method in Theology*, pp. 235ff. For a treatment of the place of imagination in this shift, see Tracy, David: *The Analogical Imagination. Christian Theology and the Culture of Pluralism* (New York: Crossroad, 1981), especially p. 562. For a parallel analysis from the point of view of liberation theology, see Enrique Dussel's treatment of the "totality" and the "other" in *Método para una filosofía de la liberacion* (Salamanca: Sígueme, 1974). pp. 188ff.

[7] For a fuller treatment of the idea of "correlation" in theology and its application to preaching, see the introduction to volume 2 of this series.

Second Sunday of the Year

Is 62:1-5
Ps 96:1-2, 2-3, 7-8, 9-10
1 Cor 12:4-11
Jn 2:1-12

Not long ago I was privileged to officiate at a wonderful wedding. I had known the groom since he was a small boy, and the bride since they had begun going out together. I knew them both to be sincere, not only in their love for each other, but also in the faith that they professed in their wedding ceremony. I had a tremendous sense of the rightness of what we were doing: not only celebrating their marriage, but doing so before God and a Christian community, in connection with the ancient words and symbols of faith.

In precisely this respect, I am sorry to say, this particular celebration stood out as exceptional. Like most priests, I have been the official witness at a great many weddings, and all too often I have very ambivalent feelings about my role. Frequently I find myself wondering about the wisdom or maturity of the couple standing before me. On many other occasions, it is painfully obvious that faith has little to do with what is going on; the church ceremony and the symbols of the sacred have no intrinsic meaning to the couple, but are merely part of the traditional way of doing it, like the white gown, the wedding march, or the ill-fitting and garish tuxedos. In this wedding, by contrast, I experienced the sense that the love of husband and wife—and of the families surrounding them—were a conscious pointing to something more: to the ultimate reality of life, to God.

If one has had an experience of such a marriage—one's own, or that of others—then one can understand the meaning of today's gospel. At least in one interpretation, the real point of the story is not the transformation of the water, but the transformation of the wedding. If this is so, then John is not simply reporting an arbitrary act of Jesus' power, which happens to have taken place on the occasion of a marriage. Rather, the marriage is of central importance to the message of the passage. Jesus transforms this wedding into a sign of God's relation to us.

For the gospel writer, Jesus is the *real* bridegroom. This theme is found explicitly in all the synoptic gospels, and is clearly implied in John. It is a continuation of the Old Testament idea (expressed in our first reading) that God is the bridegroom, the husband of his people Israel. It is typical of John's gospel that we are invited to see a contrast between appearance and reality; between physical things or events and a deeper level to which they point for those who have faith. Thus, in the passage with the Samaritan woman, physical water is contrasted with the "living" water; in the miracle of the loaves physical bread is contrasted with the "real" bread of Christ; and here, the bridegroom of Cana is contrasted with the real, spiritual bridegroom, Jesus.

The whole incident of the wedding then becomes a symbol of a deeper level of being. It signifies the "Kingdom of God," which is frequently compared to a great wedding banquet. (It is in this symbolic context that we can understand the extraordinary abundance produced by Jesus' miracle; six water jars would hold over 120 gallons!)

Perhaps what is most significant for us about this symbolism, however, is not the particular content, but the very fact of the Christian conviction that such earthly realities can be a sign of ultimate reality, can tell us something positive about the mystery of being. One of the great sayings of Buddhism is that "nothing from here [the world] can pass over to there [*nirvâṇa*]"; and the great mystical negative theology of Hinduism is based on the principle of "not this, not this"— God is unlike everything of our experience. In the religious stories of these traditions marriage is frequently used as a sign of the illusory nature of the world and of its impermanent, transitory character, utterly unlike spiritual reality.

For Christ and for the Christian, however, the ultimately real is not the negation of life, but its transcendent fulfillment, in which it comes to a new and deeper meaning. Christianity is moved by the conviction that we already have an experience of God; that God is in the world, in life, drawing us to himself.

The bridegroom, the wedding, the banquet can be signs of God because life itself is "sacramental"; it can point beyond itself, because it already contains and makes present what it points to. It is in the context of this "sacramental" vision of life that the church's sacraments occur. In our gospel reading, the miraculous wine on one level refers to the eucharist (the servants at the banquet are called διάκονοι—"deacons"; as the word is unusual in the context, we may take it as a clear indication of the intention of a liturgical understanding); what we are doing now is what the miracle of Cana is about. But the sacramental reality of our celebration depends upon our seeing and living the deeper reality of all life as the "marriage" of God with his people; seeing that what life is about is exactly what true marriage signifies: the unselfish and joyous giving of self to the other; the making of the other's life into one's own; living in and for love.

Third Sunday of the Year

Neh 8:2-4, 5-6, 8-10
Ps 19:8, 9, 10, 15
1 Cor 12:12-30
Lk 1:1-4, 4:14-21

The gospel of Luke is the main source of readings for the Sundays of the "C" cycle, and today's reading is intended to give us an introduction to its basic theme and message. What we have heard—after the evangelist's brief personal introduction, and skipping over the subsequent infancy narrative—is frequently called the "program discourse" of Luke, since it succinctly summarizes what this evangelist sees as the essential pattern of Jesus' ministry, epitomized in the fulfillment of the prophecy of Isaiah on which he preaches in the synagogue.

Our perception of the meaning of the passage is heightened by the contrast provided by our first reading, which documents the "birth of Judaism"—that is, the beginnings of the Jewish religion as we now know it, after the return from the Exile in Babylon (583 B.C.). Nehemiah was the governor under the Persian empire which had freed the Jews to return home and gave them their religious liberty. What takes place in this reading is the decisive act for the subsequent spirituality of Judaism: the proclamation of the Pentateuch. From this time forward, Israel officially has a Sacred Scripture; Judaism becomes a "religion of the Book." The origins of the scriptures, of course, were ancient; but it was only during the Exile that the ritual precepts of the Law were given definitive form, and it is the proclamation of these legal norms as the center of

12

Jewish life that marks "Judaism" as a new phase in Israelite history. It is characterized above all by devotion to the Torah. The new national life initiated under Nehemiah would have its source, not in the unpredictable movements of the spirit, as in the religion of the prophets, but in a detailed holy way of life firmly revealed by God himself: the Law.

In contrast, Luke portrays the basic message of Jesus as the announcement of the activity of God's spirit. Jesus does not merely read the scriptures, but turns them into a proclamation that God's kingdom has arrived in himself, the man of the spirit, bringing amnesty and release, healing and liberation. The whole rest of the gospel is the working out of this theme.

The opposition between the first and third readings is not merely to be thought of as a case of "progress," as though Jesus' preaching—and its continuation in Christianity—overcame the religion of the Law in the same way that Nehemiah's Judaism was a "development" over the pre-Exilic period. Rather, we confront here a perennial problem and conflict within religion: spirit versus law, change against stability, prophecy in tension with institution. Christianity itself has felt over the centuries the need to give concrete and stable form to the workings of the spirit; and has had to face the danger of stifling its own basic dynamism. There is evidence that the church today is undergoing a period of consolidation after the renewal of the Second Vatican Council. There is the danger in some quarters of rejecting the basic spirit of that renewal by making the council itself the basis of a new legalism, by codifying, institutionalizing, stabilizing to such an extent that there is a danger of losing what is most important: the openness to the transcendent.

This tension is not, however, merely a problem of "the institution." It affects the life of each believer. We have received the sacraments of the spirit—baptism and confirmation; but would we be comfortable in saying, "the spirit of the Lord is upon me," to do the things that Jesus proclaims: bring good news to the poor, release captives, enlighten the blind? Have these sacraments become merely rituals of belonging to a social tradition? The eucharist itself is supposed to mean a transformation by the spirit: not only the transformation of our "gifts" of bread and wine, but the transformation of the assembly itself, so that we can be sent forth into the world "to love and serve the Lord."

In the last analysis, is our religion—our *personal* religion— centered on the spirit, or on the Law? Is it a liberation, or a new kind of enslavement? It is hard to say, if we look only at ourselves, at our interior lives, but we can judge by the degree to which our lives create freedom and bring good news to others.

Fourth Sunday of the Year

Jer 1:4–5, 17–19
Ps 71:1–2, 3–4, 5–6, 15–17
1 Cor 12:31–13:13
Lk 4:21–30

"Amour, j'ai entendu tant de fois ton nom!"*

Coventry Patmore's exclamation might well express the state of us all: we have heard "love" so frequently named and spoken of, in so many contexts, that the word is in danger of becoming so commonplace as to lose any real evocative power. One can "love" ice cream or one's parents. The same word is used to cover sexual passion or unselfish benevolence, vague good-feeling toward others or the most committed devotion to God.

In this context, we might do well to attend closely to the great description of love in today's second reading. St. Paul's language has the advantage—lost in translation—of making a distinction between several forms of "love." Paul's concern here is not with erotic love [ἔρος *(eros)*—desire], nor with the sentiment that joins friends and family [φιλία *(filia)*—friendship, affection], but with the specific virtue of self-giving concern for others which the early church saw as the center of Christ's and its own life and message [ἀγάπη *(agape)*].

The community at Corinth to which Paul writes was riven with dissension and competition regarding the spiritual gifts of its members. Paul tells them that they should aspire to

* "Love, how many times have I heard thy name!"

15

the greater spiritual gifts—which for him are those which are oriented precisely to the building up of the community. Better than all other charisms, therefore, is love: greater than the ability to perform miracles or prophesy or speak in tongues, greater than material generosity, greater than courageous self-sacrifice. All of these, without love, are worth nothing.

What, then, is "love"? St. Paul does not give a definition, but describes how this attitude manifests itself in act. Our translation unfortunately misses the rhetorical power of the conclusion of Paul's description: "There is no limit to love's forbearance, to its trust, its hope, its power to endure." What the original says is: "Love covers over all [πάντα στένει], believes all [πάντα πιστεύει], hopes for all [πάντα ἐλπίζει], endures all [πάντα ὑπομένει]." Each phrase marks a progression in love's depth.

"Love covers over all." That is, love covers over our neighbors' faults; it does not point out others' sins to reprove them, but covers over everything with patience.

"Love believes all." Paul is not speaking here of faith in God, but faith in our brothers and sisters. Love wishes to interpret everything in the best light, wishes to believe the best possible of others. In contrast to cynicism, love believes in the goodness of humanity.

"Love hopes for all." Even when it meets with undeniable evidence of evil, love does not abandon the evildoer, but hopes for conversion; love is convinced of the ultimate triumph of goodness.

"Love endures all." Even where there is no hope left of goodness, where love meets with ingratitude and maliciousness in return, it does not change; love does not return evil for evil, but instead endures all, accepting even our neighbor's burden in sacrifice of self.

Paul concludes: "Love never comes to an end." For by love, we live already in the world of eternity; we live by the values of God himself. Other gifts are immature and incomplete; they belong to our spiritual childhood. But love is mature and final; it is of the very nature of eternity.

It is this reality which we celebrate in our eucharist. Not that we already possess that love which covers all, believes all, hopes all, endures all; to hear this message is to be challenged to become what we have heard. Yet this very love does already dwell in our hearts, perhaps only as a small flame. But in the contemplation of the love with which we have been loved, that flame may grow to become the blaze which will give light and warmth to the cold and darkened world.

Fifth Sunday of the Year

Is 6:1–2, 3–8
Ps 138:1–2, 2–3, 4–5, 7–8
1 Cor 15:1–11
Lk 5:1–11

I am sure there would be few of us who as children did not play the game "hide-and-seek." We probably still have a stirring of reaction on hearing the cry, "ready or not, here I come!" Whether we were well or ill prepared, whether we had found a good hiding place or were still half-exposed, the game was on. My memories of that feeling were evoked when I read today's gospel. It indicates to us, I think, that Christianity is a religion of "ready or not."

What I mean by this may become more apparent through considering a contrasting religious attitude. In the sacred scriptures of Buddhism, we read the following description of the Buddha Gautama's reaction after he attained spiritual enlightenment:

> Observing all sentient beings with the eyes of a Buddha, he felt deep compassion for them; he wished to purify those whose minds had been lost in false views arising from hatred, greed, and folly.
>
> But how could liberation, which is so exquisite and profound, be expressed in words? It may be better not to give out my thoughts (he said to himself), and so he remained silent and at peace.

Gautama realizes that the message of spiritual liberation is hard; few people want to hear it; most are not ready for it;

18

and so he decides not to preach. It is only when the god Brahma comes to plead with him that he is persuaded that there are people who can receive his message. Even when the Buddha does preach, however, he waits for others to come to him. He does not force his message on anyone. His disciples all take the initiative in seeking him out and choosing to follow him. Moreover, in his preaching the Buddha practices *upâya*, or "skill in means:" he always adapts his message to the level of what his audience can accept; he does not go beyond their capacity.

In contrast, Jesus' attitude seems to be, "ready or not! ..." His disciples are not volunteers; they are commanded to follow him, even if they are not prepared, even if they have not understood the message, even if they are sinners. There is an urgency to Jesus' mission and message that is totally lacking in those of the Buddha.

This points to a radical difference in contexts. Buddhism takes for granted the doctrine of reincarnation. People will keep being reborn in earthly lives until they are fit for *Nirvâna*. They will only meet God when they are ready for him; and this may take many lifetimes of purification and preparation.

For biblical religion, on the other hand, there is a basic conviction that "this is it." There is only one life, and we will meet God whether we are prepared or not. Therefore Jesus does not wait or hesitate; he confronts people and shakes them up. "Ready or not," the Kingdom of God is here; now is the time, the only time, for conversion; you must follow, even if not prepared.

Our present Christian life, including the celebration of the sacraments, also has an element of "ready or not." How many of us are really "disposed" for the celebration of the eucharist? We come to church only half-attentive, and generally with no preparation. The same is true of Christian life as a whole. The church is not perfect in understanding the message it preaches, not prepared for the circumstances it must meet, not totally ready to follow Jesus in discipleship. Yet this is where and when we are called to follow and to meet God, despite our flaws.

There is, then, a double message to be heard. First, if you are not ready, then get ready! This is our only chance; the game is on. Second, even in our failure, our unreadiness, God wants us and will have us. We cannot even look to our faults and unpreparedness as an excuse. We must heed the call: "follow me"—ready or not.

Sixth Sunday of the Year

Jer 17:5–8
Ps 1:1–2, 3, 4, 6
1 Cor 15:12, 16–20
Lk 6:17, 20–26

A good friend of mine recalls that his Irish mother had a saying that she frequently repeated: "You never laugh but you cry"—meaning: be suspicious of happiness; don't be lulled into a sense of security by good fortune. If things are going well now, you can expect misery to arrive soon.

This pessimistic attitude toward the world—the idea that happiness must be paid for in suffering, as though to maintain some kind of cosmic balance, or that there is a sort of quota of pain that everyone must undergo, might sound to many like a familiar Christian viewpoint; and, indeed, it might be thought by some to be a reasonable extrapolation from today's gospel.

Luke's redaction of the "Sermon on the Plain" differs from Matthew's corresponding "Sermon on the Mount" in several respects. While both obviously have the same source, Matthew's version [Mt 5:3–12]—the one probably more familiar to us—spiritualizes the beatitudes, emphasizing interior attitudes. Luke, however, does not speak of the poor "in spirit" or those hungering "for righteousness," as does Matthew. Luke is thinking of the materially poor, the physically hungry and weeping: *they* shall obtain satisfaction in God's kingdom. Furthermore, Luke alone adds to the beatitudes a series of "woes": those who are now rich or full or happy or

21

well-received will have the tables turned on them, and will in the future suffer.

While this may sound superficially like a sort of cosmic justice, it can only be so if one is convinced that God insists upon a certain degree of suffering as the basic price of exist-ence which everyone must pay either now or later (although the balance is highly questionable if one group suffers "only" on earth, and the other for eternity). Furthermore, if inter-preted in this way, the notion goes counter to the entire morality of the New Testament, which ties our eternal fate not to our external circumstances, but to our interior dis-positions and the actions that flow from them.

But, if the woes that are predicted cannot be simply an automatic and amoral reversal of fortune, are they then to be seen as the punishment for sin? Is Luke then saying that—contrary to the predominant theology of the Old Testament—the rich and happy of this world are necessarily *evil,* and *therefore* will be sorry when God's justice arrives? Corre-spondingly, are we to think that poverty and misfortune are necessarily signs of virtue? Is life in this world supposed to be a "vale of tears" for the good, to be recompensed by happi-ness (only) in the hereafter?

Such ideas—at least in so simplistic a form—do not, I think, fit with our experience, nor with our Christian hope for the world. The unhappy are not always good, nor are the good always unhappy. Christians—from St. Paul onward—have claimed to experience joy and peace in Christ, on the earth and using its blessings, in the present life, as a sign of our future with God. What, then, are we to make of these beatitudes and woes?

Jesus proclaims a blessing upon those who have failed to find fulfillment in the world. But clearly this is obviously not a benediction of poverty or hunger or misery in themselves, as though a particular material condition were the guarantee of salvation (were such the case, the imperative to improve the lot of the poor and hungry would make no sense). What Jesus is saying is that those who experience need have an advantage in approaching God's kingdom; they are open to its promise of fulfillment, precisely because they have not found satisfaction in the present world. They experience an emptiness which is open to be filled up by God. (Hence, Matthew's making poverty and hunger into spiritual qualities is, to this extent, in line with Jesus' meaning.)

The authenticity of the "woes" (that is, whether they were actually pronounced by Jesus) is called into question by contemporary scholars. Since they are simply the reversal of the beatitudes, some think that they might be an extension added by Luke or by the early church. At the same time, they are clearly in accord with a line of thought which undoubtedly does stem from Jesus: namely, the idea that riches are dangerous, and can be an obstacle to the acceptance of God's kingdom (cf. Mk 10:23–31, Mt 19:23–30, Lk 18:24–30; Mt 6:19–21, Lk 12:33–34; Mt 6:24, Lk 16:13). The reason for this is plain: those who are satisfied here and now, or who spend all their energy striving for such satisfaction, are already "filled," and have no desire for the fulfillment of God's kingdom. Jesus is convinced that it is easier to have the qualities that lead to real happiness in God if one is not taken up with the false gods of material possessions and worldly success.

What do these "woes" have to say to us, who are for the most part not hungry or poor, and who lead lives of comparative happiness? Certainly they must serve as a reminder and a warning. Clearly, wealth and earthly satisfactions are not *per se* evil. But the Christian will approach them with a certain reserve: not because (as pessimistic fatalism would have it) good fortune and happiness always portend a reversal by malicious fate, but because they can ensnare and delude us.

A repeated theme of Pope John Paul II has been that the

decline of faith in the prosperous Western nations is linked to a "materialistic" attitude. And have we not seen evidence of this in our own experience? It is perhaps rare that people turn away from the practice of faith because they explicitly recognize that it would be hypocritical to profess Christian values while pursuing their actual "life-style"; more frequently, people simply "lose interest": what the church preaches and cares about has increasingly little to do with their ambitions and goals. Have we not seen people who have become more callous, less caring, more self-centered, as they became more prosperous? Have we not seen success create new "needs," so that one-time luxuries become necessities, and people become enslaved rather than freed by their possessions? (It is a curious and significant fact that the poor are—proportionately—more generous than the wealthy in their donations to the church; does this have something to do with values?)

Of course, it need not be so; riches can be used to improve the world, to feed the hungry, to make this a better place for all to live; earthly happiness can be the foretaste and sign of God's kingdom. But this depends upon our being open to that dimension which is always "beyond" the self and its immediate satisfactions; a dimension open not only to God, but to all those with whom God identifies himself. We must fill the hungry, console the weeping, aid the persecuted and rejected; for we are not only to live in expectation of God's kingdom, but are also to be his instruments in bringing it about.

Seventh Sunday of the Year

1 Sam 26:2, 7–9, 12–13, 22–23
Ps 103:1–2, 3–4, 8, 10, 12–13
1 Cor 15:45–49
Lk 6:27–38

An article in the news tells of a Palestinian professor in Israel who has been sentenced for writing an article calling for Arab "resistance" to the Israeli occupation of the West Bank. His defense argued that "resistance" can mean many things; it can be peaceful, and need not be illegal. The professor was nevertheless convicted, the court accepting the prosecutor's charge that his article was an incitement to violence.

The account has little that is remarkable about it; it is the kind of story we have unfortunately come to expect from that tragic part of the world. The professor is looked on as an enemy by the Israeli court, and as a hero by the Palestinians. But what if the professor had written an article calling for *non*-resistance to Israeli rule? Many of his own people would no doubt think him either a fool or a traitor or both. Or, to expand the example, what if a Catholic professor in Belfast urged his compatriots not to oppose British occupation in Northern Ireland, and to accept the dominance of the Protestant majority there? Or suppose someone had advised citizens of Nazi-occupied France not to resist Hitler's troops? For that matter, what do we think of those colonists who rejected the Declaration of Independence, and thought that Americans should accept the colonialist policies of the English government in 1776?

I do not mean to imply that all of these cases are the same, except in one respect: that many of us would probably find, at least in some instances, not only that resistance would be the proper and moral response, but also that non-resistance would be immoral, cowardly, and irresponsible.

This perspective sharpens the challenge of today's gospel message. Israel in Jesus' time was occupied by the Romans. A "national liberation movement" was going on, and was being fiercely repressed. In this context, Jesus' teaching about loving one's enemies, turning the other cheek, and not resisting the evildoer goes not only against spontaneous human instincts on the personal level; not only against the national aspirations of his people; but against a whole religious ideology as well. For the Jews believed their nation to be divinely established and ordained, and to have a triumphant destiny as God's kingdom under his anointed, the Messiah.

Of course, Jesus' sayings are not intended as a political program—although they do manifest a conception of how God's rule is to be established which is at odds with the commonly accepted political one of his day; nor do they even constitute the general norms of an ethical philosophy, from which we could deduce the specific rules of our private or societal conduct. They are, rather, examples of the attitude which characterizes God's kingdom.

But if we cannot take these sayings as a simple and universally applicable guide for conduct, it does not follow that they are not to be taken seriously. It is precisely their fundamental spirit which must inform all our decisions and conduct. When we return evil for evil, then the reign of evil has been extended; when we return good for evil—whatever particular form the "good" may take in a particular instance in a world where the ideal good is seldom an option—then God's kingdom is advanced.

In the great Hindu religious classic, the *Bhagavad-Gîtâ*, a warrior prince has scruples about entering into battle for his throne, since it would mean the slaughter of many people, including members of his own family who are among the enemy. The supreme God Vishnu appears and teaches him that he must love God as his only goal; but, at the same time, he must also perform the duty of his state in life, which is to be a warrior. The love of God does not change the earthly state of things; it only detaches the heart from them. For Christians, in contrast, the love of God is meant to change the human situation. God's reign of peace, love, and justice is meant to begin here and now, among us. This obviously does not happen all at once, and the gospel does not give us a specific program for its accomplishment. We are not freed from the need for intelligence and prudence in making our moral and political choices, but we are given a vision to guide us—that of returning good for evil, until it is possible to transform the world and replace evil with good.

Eighth Sunday of the Year

Sir 27:4–7
Ps 92:2–3, 13–14, 15–16
1 Cor 15:54–58
Lk 6:39–45

There probably comes a time in every person's life when he or she begins to ask the questions: "Have I done any good in my life? Have I made a difference? Is the world better for my having lived in it?" Or even: "Is my life worthwhile? Is it worth going on?"

From the point of view of religious hope, one might also pose the questions this way: "Is this life worthy of being eternalized? Is there something here that is so valid, so valuable, that it should endure forever? Or would it be just as well, from the cosmic point of view, if this particular bit of ego were annihilated after its brief earthly span?"

Christian religion teaches that there is—or can be—something precious and unlimitedly valuable about each human life; something worthy of God. It inculcates in us the hope of eternity. But that hope is tied to a condition: the free achievement on our part of the goodness with which we are gifted by creation. The Matthean parallel to today's gospel not only says that "Every good tree produces good fruit" (Mt 7:17), but also that "every tree that does not produce good fruit is taken out and thrown into the fire" (Mt 7:19). The gospel knows no purely "internal" virtue; goodness must have an effect on the world, must be productive. (This should not be understood in the sense that we "earn" God's love by our good acts; rather, that effective human goodness is the

result and sign of the real presence and acceptance of that
love.)

What, then, have we accomplished? What do our lives
have to show as the sign of God's effective love present and
working through us? How is the world different and better
for our having been in it?

In thinking of this theme my mind continually returns
to the concluding words written by George Eliot about the
heroine of her masterly novel, *Middlemarch:*

> ... Certainly those determining acts of her life were
> not ideally beautiful. They were the mixed result of
> young and noble impulses struggling amidst the con-
> ditions of an imperfect social state, in which great feel-
> ings will often take the aspect of error, and great faith the
> aspect of illusion. For there is no creature whose inward
> being is so strong that it is not greatly determined by
> what lies outside it.
> ... But the effect of her being on those around her
> was incalculably diffusive: for the growing good of the
> world is partly dependent on unhistoric acts; and that
> things are not so ill with you and me as they might have
> been, is half owing to the number who lived faithfully a
> hidden life, and rest in unvisited tombs.

It is not always easy to discern the concrete effect of
goodness; it is frequently not of great name. But, as Eliot
remarks, the good is "incalculably diffusive," even when unnoticed and anonymous. The "good fruit" of a Christian life
may seem small in itself, but its true effect can only be known
in the light of the larger collaboration toward the good of
which it is a humble part. We may not see any great results
but, as St. Paul assures the Corinthians, "You know your toil
is not in vain when it is done in the Lord" (second reading).

Working "in the Lord" of course depends upon our interiority, the disposition of our "heart" (gospel). But good disposition is not enough of itself; good will can also produce objectively evil effects if it is not accompanied by intelligence and understanding of the situation in which we act. Thus the Christian is called both to interiority and to communion: to acting as part of a community which reflects upon the world in the light of faith. Such community not only gives direction to our acts, but enlarges their scope.

This enlargement is one of the purposes of our coming together here. Many people complain—no doubt with justice—that they are not nourished by the liturgy; that the preaching is poor, the ceremony ill-performed. These are important failings, and we as the church must address them. But there is another level of nourishment that does not depend upon preaching and ritual. Our very presence together should be for each a sign of hope; a sign that we are not alone, not restricted to our little lives and efforts. When we come together in the eucharist we see our individual acts not merely as "ours," but as part of a larger collaboration; we can see the "good fruit" of our own lives in the light of the building of the "body" of the Lord.

Ninth Sunday of the Year

1 Kgs 8:41–43
Ps 117:1, 2
Gal 1:1–2, 6–10
Lk 7:1–10

According to Plato, the last words of the philosopher Socrates before he drank the deadly cup of hemlock were to his friend Crito: "I owe a cock to Aesculapius; do not neglect to pay the debt." In saying that he owed a sacrifice of thanksgiving to the god of healing, Socrates was expressing his conviction that his impending death was, in fact, a healing, the "cure" for the illness of life itself. Bodily life in the world is regarded as a kind of exile or imprisonment for the soul, which belongs elsewhere, in a non-material heavenly sphere. Hence, death is seen as liberation, an act of mercy.

Quite a different view of things is presupposed by the New Testament writers and the Christian tradition. In today's gospel we hear the beginning of Luke's account of a series of works of mercy of Jesus: healing, raising the dead to life, comforting the sorrowing, forgiving sins. The power of God in Jesus does not take people out of the world to a better place; rather, it makes the world right; it transforms it into the Kingdom of God. Hence, for Jesus the desire for healing, for life in the world, is continuous with the attitude of faith: trust in God's loving power to restore and re-create the world.

It is for this attitude that the centurion is praised and held up as a model. His message to Jesus shows supreme confidence. He understands that the power at work in Jesus is that of authority; there is no need for Jesus to work, to do battle against evil, like an exorcist; no need even for him to be present. Moreover, the centurion's hope in Jesus is not based on his own worthiness; he makes no claim upon Jesus (as the elders, by contrast, do: "He deserves this favor from you"); his request is based solely on his confidence in Jesus' goodness. He is both supremely confident and humble. As he says in his message, he knows what power and authority are; what is unsaid, but presupposed, is that he also knows what compassion and love are. He loves the Jewish people, and he asks for healing, not for himself, but for his servant. His faith is that he expects to find in Jesus both power and love; and his hope is not in vain.

The church paraphrases the centurion's words in the prayer that we recite in every eucharist immediately before communion: "Lord, I am not worthy to receive you, but only say the word and I shall be healed."

Clearly, the words are meant to express the attitude of faith: humble confidence in the power of God in Jesus, still at work in the world, and able to touch our lives. But what do we mean by saying that we will be "healed" by Jesus' word? Not, like Socrates, that we shall be simply taken out of earthly life; nor that we hope to regain a merely physical well-being, like the centurion's servant. The context in which we say these words is the eucharist, in which we remember and give thanks for the death and rising of Jesus, and express our participation in those events. It is they that interpret our desire for "healing"—the transformation of our lives, in the world, into resurrected life, the foretaste of eternal life; the rising of love and hope out of the sickness of egotism, despair, and indifference.

Like Socrates, we also offer a thanksgiving to God for the healing we experience. But just as our idea of healing in Christ is different from the Platonic flight from the world, so also is our sacrifice different from the offering of external gifts. It is the healing itself, the new life in us, the attitude of faith and love, transforming the world, which is itself both the healing and the thanksgiving.

Tenth Sunday of the Year

1 Kgs 17:17–24
Ps 30:2, 4, 5–6, 11, 12, 13
Gal 1:11–19
Lk 7:11–17

In my opinion the most profound and beautiful film of the Japanese master, Akira Kurosawa, is not any of the great epics (*The Seven Samurai, Kagemusha, Ran*) for which he is famous, but a much lesser-known work that is quite outside his usual samurai genre and does not even take place in Japan. Its title, *Dersu Uzala*, is the name of a Siberian hunter who actually lived toward the end of the last century, and whose life is chronicled by one of the Russian explorers for whom he served as a guide during the period of the colonization of that vast region. The film explores not only the friendship which springs up between these two men, but also the difference between their ways of life. The Russian officer is a man of the city, a representative of civilization; Dersu is a child of nature, at home with its wildness and beauty, at one with all creatures.

At one point in the story, one of the Russian soldiers on the expedition, having finished his meal, throws the leftovers into the campfire. Dersu quickly thrusts his hand into the fire and pulls the food out. In broken Russian, he scolds the soldier, asking why he threw food away; if he left it, someone would come along to eat it. From the remote hilltop where they are sitting, the soldier looks out upon hundreds of miles of uninhabited wilderness. He laughs. "Who can come?," he asks. Dersu replies, "Mouse come; wolf come. . . ."

For the woodsman, the animals are "someone" just as people are. He sees spirits everywhere, not only in humans. Like St. Francis in the "Canticle of the Sun," he feels a kinship with all beings; all are brothers and sisters, and his compassion extends to all.

Today's gospel should also be read as a call to compassionate solidarity. At first sight, we are dealing with a miracle story, consciously echoing the Old Testament in order to make a point about Jesus' identity. Like Elijah and Elisha, Jesus raises the dead; indeed, the scene in the gospel purposely evokes the miracle of the prophet Elijah (first reading), who also raised a widow's son and "gave him back to his mother." This evocation of the past explains the reaction of the crowd; Jesus, like Elijah and Elisha, is a "great prophet," one in whom God comes to his people, because he does as they had done.

Luke's emphasis, however, is on the compassion of Jesus. It is notable that our attention is drawn, not to the young man who is brought back to life, but to his mother: Jesus is "moved with pity on seeing *her;*" and the climax of the miracle is not the man's receiving back his life, but the mother's receiving back her son. Luke is not interested in the miraculous restoration of life, but in Jesus' feeling and acting in solidarity with the suffering of the woman. It is not a momentary escape from death which is significant (for all must die to be with God); it is rather the lesson about living which is important. Jesus preaches a life of active love of neighbor; here he puts it into practice.

Luke would have us understand that such compassion represents the highest relation to God. It is the true heart of religion, beyond the Law; it overcomes the pollution of death. (Note that Jesus, like the Good Samaritan in the parable, risks contamination by his action. According to the Law, touching a cadaver or even a tomb made a person "unclean," alienated from the community.* For Jesus, however, compassion is a higher "law" and a higher communion.) Compassion is the love of neighbor "as oneself"; for we take the point of view of the other as our own, we feel for the other as we would for ourselves. The ability and willingness to feel another's pain and need, and to act to heal them, is also the highest reflection of the divine nature; for so Jesus teaches God is toward us.

The universal love and solidarity taught by the gospel are clearly oriented to the world of humanity. We find no nature mysticism or animism in the New Testament or, for that matter, in the biblical tradition as a whole. The legends of the Buddha recount that in one of his incarnations he gave his body to feed a hungry tiger, so great was his compassion for all living things. For the Buddhist—as for Kurosawa's hunter—there is ultimately no difference between humanity and nature; it is the very same life that manifests itself in different forms. We would look in vain for such ideas in the Bible. Here, humanity is seen as the master of creation, the special image of God. Yet it has become clear, particularly in our day, that compassionate openness to each other must include care for our world as well; when we feel toward each other an attitude of reverence and concern rather than manipulation and domination, it can only be on the basis of recognizing our common createdness as God's children; and such recognition will lead us to love, and not merely use, all our fellow creatures.

* Numbers 19:11, 16.

Eleventh Sunday of the Year

2 Sam 12:7–10, 13
Ps 32:1–2, 5, 7, 11
Gal 2:16, 19–21
Lk 7:36 – 8:3

Why do people no longer go to confession?

It is a fact that the regular individual confession of sins to a priest, once a hallmark of Roman Catholic practice, has radically declined, even among devout churchgoers. The reasons for the decline, however, are not immediately clear. Many people will attribute the change in practice to the fact that the church today—i.e., after the Second Vatican Council—is "less strict" than it used to be. But the same observation could be made with approval or disapproval; and it is not obvious whether this change is to be looked at as a positive or a negative phenomenon.

An optimistic view might see the decline in confession as a sign of the success of post-Vatican II catechetics. It might be argued that modern Catholics see less need for confession because they realize that it is not necessary to confess their sins each time they wish to receive the eucharist; because the image of a loving and tender God has replaced that of a stern and demanding power; because Catholics are theologically more sophisticated, and recognize that there are other means for the forgiveness of sin; because, finally, a combination of psychological and theological insight has given us a new sense of just what sin is and what it is not, allowing Catholics to overcome the negative self-image, the all-pervasive sense of guilt and unworthiness, that was once inculcated in them.

A negative view might see the same phenomena in rather a different light, pointing to a loss of the sense of sin itself, and seeing this as a capitulation to the more general "permissiveness" of our society, an adoption of the uncritical self-acceptance and lack of responsibility that are signs of social and moral decline. Moreover, it might be pointed out, regular confession was for the laity not merely a sacrament of forgiveness, but was the most common form of spiritual direction. Its decline could signify not only the loss of a sense of sin, but also the loss of a sense of the need for spiritual progression and/or a loss of confidence in the clergy as spiritual guides.

Beyond the question of sacramental confession, therefore, there lies a more profound issue: what place does—or should—the consciousness of "sin" and "forgiveness" have in the spiritual life of a Christian? Are these marginal realities, or are they at the very center of Christian consciousness? Is the need to be continually forgiven a sign of a psychologically unhealthy self-concept, or is it a basic spiritual reality? Do we need to be delivered from our *sense* of guilt, or from *guilt* itself?

An examination of the message of today's gospel may help to clarify our perspective. The passage first of all seems to present two opposite points of view regarding love and forgiveness. Jesus' parable implies that the sinful woman—like the grateful debtor who owed a vast sum—loves much because she has been forgiven much. In his subsequent explanation to his host, however, Jesus seems to reverse the message: the woman has been forgiven much because she loves much. Jesus seems, in effect, to be saying that the woman's love is both the cause and the effect of her being forgiven.

This becomes more understandable when we contrast the attitude of the host. He does not think that he needs forgiveness; he is "just." Hence he does not receive Jesus with love, neglecting even the ordinary courtesies of society (having his feet washed, greeting him with a kiss). He is not looking for forgiveness, and therefore cannot receive Jesus and his message with an open and expectant heart. Yet the implication of Jesus' parable is that he, too, is a debtor— although to a lesser degree—who is unable to repay. Jesus' message of God's generous forgiveness applies to him as well. Because he does not wish to be forgiven by God, the self-righteous Pharisee misses the gift of God's love; and in turn he closes himself to the love of others. The sinful woman, in the recognition of her need and the hope of God's mercy, loves; that love is itself the event of God's forgiveness. Hence, it is as true to say that she is forgiven because she loves, as that she loves because she is forgiven.

The point for us seems to be that the need for God's "forgiveness" is universal; that we must acknowledge our need, our "indebtedness," in order to open ourselves to his love. Does this mean that the Christian must, after all, live with the conviction that we are all "guilty"?

It must first of all be understood that there is no question of rejecting the valid insights of modern psychology about the limitations of our responsibility or of modern theology about the centrality of God's love. There can be no question of a return to an anxious and guilt-ridden mentality that contradicts the freedom and joy of the "good news" itself. But the reception of that good news itself depends upon the recognition of certain insights about ourselves and our situation which constitute the Christian notion of sin: that the wrongs of the world are not *simply* due to inevitability or accident or ignorance; that we are to some greater or lesser extent—through our action or our *inaction*—responsible; that we are loved by God, and that the most fundamental desire of our being is the return of that love, so that the evils we do and the good we fail to do are contrary to a more fundamental dynamism toward perfection; and that, therefore, our lives are radically open to "forgiveness," the healing and expansion of our fundamental goodness by the ever-present affirmation of God.

Whatever may be the future of sacramental confession, therefore, there can be no doubt that the "forgiveness of sins" remains central to Christian consciousness. Authentic Christian life is never a secure possession, but is always also a turning away from inauthenticity and toward a fuller and more universal love. We will always need signs to express and realize the reality of the move from egotism and alienation to communion and love. And the primary expression of that reality is, in fact, what we celebrate here and now, and in every eucharist, when we commemorate the body broken and the blood poured out "so that sins may be forgiven."

Twelfth Sunday of the Year

Zech 12:10–11
Ps 63:2, 3–4, 5–6, 8–9
Gal 3:26–29
Lk 9:18–24

If one looks around most churches on a Sunday morning, one notices a conspicuous lack of a particular age group. In most congregations one can see large numbers of older and middle-aged people; a great many families with their young children; and at least a fair sprinkling of early teenagers. But one seldom sees many unmarried young adults: people from their late teens to their late twenties are severely under-represented. This is, of course, a generalization. On many college campuses, for example, one can find impressive examples of youth involved and committed not only to liturgy but also to personal prayer and social action. Still, most would probably agree that such situations are atypical; and when the active young people from the Newman clubs and campus ministries are spread out in their home parishes, they are seen to be spread very thin indeed.

What accounts for the lack of involvement of this age group (which is, of course, the group upon which the church traditionally relied for vocations to the priesthood and religious life) in worship and religion in general? Clearly it is not simply age in itself; in Poland and in some third-world countries the churches are full of young adults. It would seem to have something specifically to do with our society.

One explanation of the phenomenon that is sometimes heard is that the church does not "offer" anything for people

41

of this age. If what is meant by this is that there are not enough special programs—dances, discussion groups, etc.—for young adults, then the explanation seems far from satisfactory; for even where such programs exist, they are generally quite unsuccessful (if success is measured in terms of attracting significant numbers). On the other hand, it is probably true that the church in America suffers from a failure of imagination in ministry in general—to every age group. Intelligent preaching, beautiful liturgy, vibrant community, engaging activities are perhaps not typical of most parishes. But even where these things are present, do they reach or appeal to the majority of young people? Do not "good" parishes experience the same gap in the makeup of the congregation?

Is it possible that it is not simply failure of imagination in presenting it, but something *intrinsic* to the Christian message which makes it unappealing to so many young people in our society once they reach the age of personal freedom?

What that "something" may be is pointed to by today's gospel. Its message, in essence, is: you cannot know Jesus without the cross. When the disciples acknowledge Jesus as the Messiah—the anointed of God, the glorious and triumphant King—he immediately corrects them with the saying about his suffering and death, and insists that his followers must embrace the same fate. The message of Christianity is about failure, suffering, death—the breakdown of the human world, and the experience or anticipation of these realities is instrinsic to knowing who Jesus is, his meaning for us, and how we are to follow him.

Of course, the scandal of the cross is a difficulty not only for the young, but in our society, it is perhaps particularly hard for them to grasp or accept. More significantly, in our society it is psychologically *possible* for them not to grasp or accept it; that is, they are to a large degree able to escape—or at least to imagine that they are doing so—from the common human realities of suffering and mortality. The ideal presented to them is that of the carefree life; and in the flush of youth, they can believe in its possibility. The young (generalizing again) do not really believe in death; they have not confronted failure; they are largely without serious responsibilities. But in order for the Christian message to make sense in a mature context, one must have come to terms with one's mortality and finitude, with the need for salvation. As the theologian Paul Tillich wrote:

> Only those who have experienced the shock of transitoriness, the anxiety in which they are aware of their finitude, the threat of non-being, can understand what the notion of God means.

To be a mature Christian, one must have encountered the tragic dimension of life, its limitations, either in oneself or in active sympathy with others. This requires either wide experience or a large-heartedness and absence of self-concern, a maturity of spirit, that would be rare in the turmoil of self-discovery of late adolescence in our society. Thus it is ultimately not surprising that the encounter with these realities is unappealing to those experiencing the vitality and immediate gratifications of young life.

But the absence of the young from the church and its issues is perhaps more an extended "sabbatical" than a rejection. Frequently it is marriage and/or parenthood which occasions a return. Again, it is not surprising that it should be the encounter with a self-sacrificing love, in which one willingly accepts to suffer with or for the sake of another, and finds in this more meaning and fulfillment, more joy than in carefree pleasure, which is the opening to the permanent validity of the Christian message. For that message is precisely that the cross and suffering are not the end or the last

word; they are—in love—the means to joy, peace, resurrection, the real "finding" of one's life.

Even the great pagan humanists knew that true fulfillment, real humanity, must include fellowship with others,
sympathy, openness to the full reality of human being, which
includes its tragedy and its end. So Lucretius wrote in his
celebrated poem, "De Rerum Natura": *hic etiam sunt lacrimae
rerum . . . et mentem mortalia tangunt* ("here"—that is, where
true human beings are found—"there are also the tears of
things, and the mind is touched by mortality . . .").

For the Christian, however, the basic attitude inspired by
the human condition is not merely one of resignation or sad
realism. The message of the resurrection means that we encounter the world with joy, thanksgiving and love. But these
always contain an element of longing—as expressed in our
psalm response. There is always the knowledge that this, the
present, is not "it," not the fulfillment or the goal; at its best, it
is a sign, and also an imperative: to rejoice in life, but also to
know that really to live means letting go of life and self, to
find a larger self and larger life in God and with each other.

Thirteenth Sunday of the Year

1 Kgs 19:16, 19–21
Ps 16:1–2, 5, 7–8, 9–10, 11
Gal 5:1, 13–18
Lk 9:51–62

In the second act of Oscar Wilde's comedy *The Importance of Being Earnest,* young Cecily Cardew asks her tutor, Miss Prism, whether the novel she had written had a happy ending. Miss Prism answers: "The good ended happily, and the bad unhappily. That is what Fiction means."

Although there have been many changes in literature since the time of the Victorian novel, examples of Miss Prism's idea of fiction still abound. Not only books but, even more powerfully, television and the movies provide us with many instances of a world facilely divided between good and bad people, and in which the former invariably triumph—often by destroying the opposition with a significant degree of overkill. (Think, for example, of James Bond or Indiana Jones).

The positive or negative psychological and cultural value of such fantasies may be debated at great length. One thing that seems certain, however, is that it is dangerous when people forget that such scenarios are indeed fiction, and begin subconsciously to believe that this is the way the world actually is—or ought to be; when they think of nations or political parties in terms of "good guys" and "bad guys"—the "good guys" naturally being "our" side; when they imagine that human problems can be solved by the annihilation of evil-doers; when they expect and demand a happy ending as a reward for virtue or at least for being on the right side.

The gospel serves as a warning to Christians against any such fictional approaches to life. In the Second Book of Kings, we are told the story of the great prophet Elijah, who calls down fire from heaven to destroy two companies of soldiers sent by the wicked King Ahaziah (2 Kgs 1:9–16). Jesus' disciples James and John wish to emulate the prophet in dealing with the Samaritans who refuse to accept their master. But Jesus is going toward his "ascension" (αναλήμψις—literally, "being taken up," i.e., to heaven; our translation gives "taken from this world"). For Luke this concept includes the whole process of Jesus' elevation to God *through* his cross, death, and resurrection; his triumph, which takes place, not by conquest or violence, but by suffering and transformation. Hence, Jesus rebukes the disciples' militant fervor on his behalf; goodness does not triumph through the annihilation of its enemies, but by redemptive love, of which the cross is the exemplar.

In Luke's gospel, Jesus' entire ministry is structured as a journey to Jerusalem, where it reaches its culmination. That culmination will not be a "happy ending"; Jesus does not "win." Yet, knowing his goal, he "firmly resolves" to undertake this journey—the necessary prelude and means to his more ultimate journey to the Father and his kingdom.

According to the gospel, that single-hearted and unflinching devotion to God's "kingdom" must also characterize those who would follow Jesus. This devotion goes beyond every other sort of purpose and loyalty. In calling his disciples to leave behind even the good of family ties, Jesus indicates the urgency of the calling. In refusing to think or act in accord with the age-old and bitter contention between Jews and Samaritans, he implicitly rejects the simple division into good and bad, us and them, as well as the vision of the kingdom in terms of earthly triumph. He presents us with a startling and perhaps unsettling challenge: to subordinate everything—both the conflicts and the joys of life—to an ultimate goal: the "reign" of God; that is, the universal and permanent fellowship of love with all people.

Fourteenth Sunday of the Year

Is 66:10–14
Ps 66:1–3, 4–5, 6–7, 16, 20
Gal 6:14–18
Lk 10:1–12, 17–20

A front-page headline in the Sunday *New York Times* recently proclaimed: "Shortage of Entrants to the Clergy Causing Alarm for U.S. Religions." The article went on to detail the shortage of candidates for ministry, not only in the Roman Catholic church, but in all major Christian and Jewish denominations. One rabbi went so far as to say that "the spiritual life of the nation is at stake," since we will in the near future be facing a serious lack of competent religious and moral leaders.

It would be natural for us in this situation to apply to ourselves the words of Jesus to the seventy-two disciples in today's gospel: "The harvest is rich, but the workers are few; therefore ask the harvest-master to send workers to his harvest."

Jesus' further comments to the missionaries may give us a hint at why we face a shortage of ministerial vocations: "I am sending you as lambs in the midst of wolves." Certainly this is not true of us in the same way that it was of first-century carriers of the gospel; the Christian community is not new and revolutionary, as it was in Jesus' time; it is not persecuted, as it was in Luke's. But it is in many respects counter-cultural; the values it preaches of peace, collaboration, love, fellowship, and so forth, are certainly not those of the rapacious competitive world of business or politics in our society. Its concerns in many ways run counter to the general vision of "success" in the world, at least as it is presented in the media.

It is certainly not surprising in a society in which the youth culture is largely permeated with drugs, unbridled sexuality, alcohol, and the pursuit of pleasure, in which material possessions are a priority, and in which educators tell us altruism and idealism have become rare, that few will opt for a vocation which demands a certain forgetfulness of self and dedication to the sharing of a spiritual vision with others.

For the minister, the priority must be the mission rather than what one gets from it. Jesus instructs the seventy-two—as he had earlier the Twelve (Lk 9:2-5)—not to take with them supplies for the journey; not to engage in anything that would impede its urgent communication. In context, this does not mean that the messenger is to do without the necessities of life; on the contrary, the message itself is to inspire generosity in those who receive it, so that the laborer receives his wage. (Later in the gospel, in fact, Luke includes a passage, in obvious reference to today's, in which Jesus asks his disciples, "when I sent you out with no purse or bag or sandals, did you lack anything?" They replied, "Nothing" [Lk 22:35]. Jesus then tells them that now—in anticipation of his rejection, culminating in the passion—they are to provide for themselves.)

Plainly the material situation of clergy or religious today cannot be simply and immediately modeled on the instructions of Jesus to the first missionaries. But it remains true that the minister lives by the generosity inspired by the message, and his or her "style of life" must be subordinated to the *purpose* of that life—a perspective quite different from the "success" orientation so prevalent in our culture (although it must also be added that the question of *happiness* in one's life and work is very different from that of "success" in material terms; in fact, those who dedicate their lives to a purpose, disregarding the reward, seem to achieve a significantly richer, more fulfilled and more human existence than those who pursue a material goal.)

Is there a prospect that the vocational situation will change? There are, of course, increasing numbers of candidates who enter the seminary later in life; but not infrequently their presumably greater maturity is counterbalanced by a certain mental rigidity that can also come with age, and in any case they are by no means sufficient in number to offset the losses. There is the possibility, held out by some, that the Roman church will open ordination to women and/or to married men; but, if we can judge by the experience of other churches who already have married and female ministers, and who are suffering the same vocational shortage, even if this were likely it would not resolve the problem except temporarily. It would seem that only a radical change of attitude and values in our social context could effect a turnaround in the prospects for ordained ministry.

But is this necessarily a tragedy for the church? Jesus says, "ask the harvest-master to send workers to his harvest." The harvest is God's; the calling to serve in it is from him. It may be that the workers he is calling are not those our past has led us to expect. And, in fact, in one sense Jesus' statement that "the workers are few" does not apply to us; for the workers in the church today are many more than in the time when clergy and religious abounded. The laity have taken over many functions that once were exclusively performed by clergy and religious: liturgical, charitable, educational. Jesus expected that the message would inspire generosity in those who heard it to support its ministers; in our day, we are seeing a more radical generosity inspired by the gospel, that of lay people taking on the tasks of those ministers. What this portends for the church in our society probably cannot be predicted; but a part of the generosity demanded of all of us is a generosity of mind: an openness to the movement of the Spirit to transform us and the church in response to the call of God's ever-imminent kingdom.

Fifteenth Sunday of the Year

Deut 30:10–14
Ps 69:14, 17, 30–31, 33–34, 36, 37
Col 1:15–20
Lk 10:25–27

In an essay question on a theology examination, I recently asked my university students to reflect on what Christianity could learn from the other great world religions we had studied. I was surprised at the number who replied that Christians could learn to observe their religion more strictly, as Muslims do. The answers sometimes showed a certain naïveté, perhaps fostered by media images—anyone who has travelled in a nominally Muslim country knows that there are very many non-observant followers of Islam, just as there are lax Christians—but it was interesting that so many students made it clear that they found value in the clear rules and discipline imposed by Islam, in contrast with what they perceived as the looseness and ambiguity of Christianity. It is frequently remarked by people of an older generation as well that the church is "not as strict as it used to be." The comment is sometimes made with disapproval, sometimes with appreciation; but in either case the focus is on the rules, the concrete norms that the church proposes for people to follow.

Now, it is of course true that many of the laws and regulations of the church have been changed, in the endeavor to bring Christian practice into line with modern times. But we would be missing the point of the contemporary renewal of the church if we were to reduce it to a matter of making the rules easier or practice "less strict." What is behind the reform is the attempt to move away from the "rule" mentality altogether, and to promote a deeper and more responsible way of thinking about the practice of faith.

Today's gospel story of the "good Samaritan" and the encounter that provokes it illustrate well the contrast between a religion centered on rules and the religion proclaimed by Jesus. For the lawyer who challenges Jesus, eternal life is apparently seen as a prize to be won by correct observance of the rules; for Jesus, on the other hand, eternal life is the life of God which has already begun in the practice of love. For the lawyer, therefore, religion is a set of obligations, leading to a reward; for Jesus, it is the living out of one's interior life.

Jesus responds to the lawyer's challenge by challenging him in return. The lawyer has asked his question in order to test Jesus' knowledge of the scriptures. Jesus shows that the lawyer already knows the answer (note that Luke, unlike the other synoptics [Mt 22:37, Mk 12:29] places the summary of the Law in the mouth of the lawyer, rather than Jesus). The rabbis had, in fact, already come to the conclusion that the love of God and neighbor was the summation of the whole Law. But they debated the limits of one's obligations. Jesus refuses to enter into this legalistic debate about how far one has to go in order to keep the rules. "Who is my neighbor?" Jesus shows that the question itself is wrong, and betrays the wrong spirit to begin with; one should rather ask, "to whom can I be a neighbor?" that is, "whom have I the opportunity of loving?"

The parable itself not only proclaims the universality of love, but contains an implicit critique of the legalist mentality. Scholars speculate that the characters of the priest and Levite are chosen for a specific purpose: we are meant to understand that their lack of compassion is directly rooted in preoccupation with the Law. If the body they saw by the wayside turned out to be a dead man, then touching him would have made them ritually unclean and unable to perform their religious functions. Jesus thus intends to shock his audience into the recognition that legalistic religion not only misses the point, but is even an obstacle to the true love of God and neighbor.

The same lesson applies to us. This is not to say that the nostalgia for a "stricter" religion necessarily betrays an ungenerous and legalistic attitude; on the contrary, it may signify the desire for a context in which to concretize and symbolize one's love. One benefit of a religion with many rules of behavior is that it makes connections: it brings one's faith into contact with daily life, and gives one a concrete sense of what to do—even if it also carries the danger that the doing may become mere formalism without heart. By contrast, many people today find their lives empty of the sacred. What this tells us is that a religion that is "less strict" is not for that reason *easier*; on the contrary, it is more demanding: it requires that we use our intelligence and imagination, that we create from within the connections of our daily lives with God, that we ask ourselves the question of the gospel: "to whom can I be a neighbor," rather than finding the rules clearly laid out to be followed. Yet, if we take seriously the message that God has actually come to us, lives in us by his Spirit, this challenge is not beyond us. As Moses tells the people in our first reading, God's command to us is not mysterious or remote; "it is something very near to you, already in your mouths and in your hearts; you have only to carry it out." Like the lawyer in the gospel, we have no difficulty in recognizing the Samaritan who acted with compassion as the one who loved his neighbor; like him we are challenged by Jesus: "Then go and do the same."

Sixteenth Sunday of the Year

Gen 18:1–10
Ps 15:2–3, 3–4, 5
Col 1:24–28
Lk 10:38–42

Anyone interested in the history of our legal tradition—or in history in general, or in learning about the church in an age very similar to our own, when new religious and secular ideas conflicted with tradition—could hardly do better for summer reading than Richard Marius' recent biography of Thomas More. Most of us probably have an image of More from the famous portrait by Hans Holbein, which already conveys a great deal of his personality, and even more from Robert Bolt's play (and later film) *A Man for All Seasons.* He looms large especially in the Catholic imagination as the model of the layman leading a life of sanctity: lawyer, scholar, successful man of the world, Lord Chancellor of England, intimate of the king and, finally, martyr for his faith.

It becomes clear from this biography that More was a very complex personality. He was a renaissance man, friend of Erasmus, author of *Utopia,* celebrating the coming of a new world and espousing a revolutionary doctrine of communism. But he was also deeply a man of the Middle Ages, especially in his religion. Although married (twice, in fact), he held to the superiority of the celibate state; although a layman, he believed in the preeminence of the clergy; although actively involved in secular life, he was convinced that the life of contemplation was better. In all this—and especially the last—he was deeply medieval. There is some irony in the fact that More is thought of as the patron saint of the laity, for he apparently regarded his state in life with some regret. He was continually drawn to a life which differed from the practical political existence he led. He recognized that such active life in the world as his was necessary; but he thought that it was so because of original sin. The ideal life for him was the religious life: more specifically, the monastic life of contemplation.

There are no doubt still many Catholics who would recognize in More's attitudes presuppositions that they share, even if they have never really thought about them explicitly. Certainly for many centuries these ideas were taken for granted by most Christians. But when one stops to think about it, one wonders exactly where such notions came from, since Jesus—unlike the Buddha, for example—did not himself withdraw from the world, was not a contemplative, left no method of meditation, and sent his followers into society rather than into monastic seclusion.

To a very large extent the Christian notion of the ideal religious life was, in fact, derived not from Jesus, but from the philosophical ideal of contemplation propounded by Aristotle. But justification for this idea was found in texts like that in today's gospel. For centuries (and until not very long ago—perhaps you have even heard such sermons, as I did in my youth), Martha and Mary were taken as symbols of two kinds or states of life. The active life (Martha) is needed, but inferior; it stems from our fallen state. The better choice is Mary's: the life of meditation on the words of the Lord.

Few texts in the New Testament have been subject to more non-contextual interpretation than this one. The meaning of the story does have to do with discipleship; it is part of a series of passages in Luke in which we are shown what it means to follow Jesus. But it has nothing to do with the exaltation of a religious contemplative life over the life of active service. Rather, it is concerned with the paramount value of hearing God's word, which is the essential condition for following Jesus. This theme is found throughout Luke's gospel: "blessed are they who hear the word of God and keep it" (Lk 11:28); "my mother and brothers are those who hear the word of God and do it" (Lk 8:21). Hearing God's word is prior even to the sacred duty of hospitality, for it serves an even deeper need and creates an even deeper communion.

Jesus is therefore pointing out to Martha that "man does not live by bread alone" (Lk 4:4). As in the episode with the Samaritan woman in John's gospel (Jn 4:4ff.), Jesus refers to a deeper nourishment of which he is the source.

This does not imply the diminishing of the practical concern for others' needs in which Martha is engaged, and of which she has become the symbol. This story follows immediately after the parable of the Good Samaritan, where we are taught that true love of neighbor means precisely concrete action. Wherever Jesus speaks of God's word, he does not talk about contemplating it, but about *doing* it. But the story of Martha is a reminder for those engaged in the service of others that our neighbors' needs are not merely material; Mary perhaps does the greater service of hospitality to Jesus by listening to him than Martha does by preparing the table.

The story also reminds us that we who would nourish others need to be nourished ourselves. The eucharist, of course, symbolizes this. We gather apart from the business of our lives to listen to God's word and be fed by his sacrament. We are reminded that however much we may act as the givers of hospitality, the preparers of the feast, we are nevertheless in the most ultimate sense its receivers. We are guests in our very existence. It is the recognition of this fact, which we encounter in God's word, that allows us to perform from the heart the service of love.

Seventeenth Sunday of the Year

Gen 18:20–23
Ps 138:1–2, 2–3, 6–7, 7–8
Col 2:12–14
Lk 11:1–13

On a visit to North Africa, I once entered a mosque in the middle of the day and encountered a remarkable experience of prayer. In the center of the courtyard a group of men was gathered, all seated on the ground in a circle; they swayed slightly from side to side as they repeated over and over, rhythmically and in unison: "l'*hamd*'ullah; l'*hamd*'ullah"— "glory to God, glory to God." The chanting must have been going on for some time already when I entered, since some of the men seemed to have entered a kind of ecstatic trance; it continued unabated for the whole time I was there.

This kind of prayer—the praise of God, simply for his own sake—is the norm for Islam. Muslim religion is based on the absoluteness of God and of his will; the word "Islam" itself means "submission" to God. The proper religious attitude is the acceptance of God's will; the proper kind of prayer is praising God for whatever he wills.

For many Christians, the notion of "prayer" that is unconsciously taken for granted is almost the opposite: not submission to God's will, but the effort to change God's will, to get him to submit to our will or fulfill our agenda. Many Christians spontaneously assume that "prayer" means asking, in the expectation or at least the hope of a response. Indeed, the very word commonly used in many of the Western languages (pray, *prier, pregare, beten,* etc.) actually means "to entreat" or "to implore." Prayer is taken to be a dialogue with God, similar to dialogue with other persons, but since in this case the person in question is believed to be all-powerful, the dialogue most frequently takes the form of attempting to convince him to use his power on the petitioner's behalf.

This kind of prayer is, of course, strongly rooted in the biblical tradition. Today's first reading, for example, presents us with the story of Abraham interceding for the cities of Sodom and Gomorrah. He pleads, cajoles, bargains with God in the effort to persuade him to spare the cities; and God answers his prayers and agrees to his conditions. (Of course, if this reading has been juxtaposed with the gospel in order to give us an example of the fruitfulness of persistence in prayer, it is somewhat ambiguous, for we all presumably remember how the story ends: there are not even ten just men to be found, and God destroys the cities after all, just as he had proposed before Abraham's intercession.)

The gospel tradition is somewhat ambivalent on the prayer of petition. On the one hand, we are encouraged to pray persistently (Lk 18:1-8) and to ask with confidence—we are even told that such prayer, made in faith, is infallible (Jn 14:13-14; 15:7). On the other hand, Jesus tells his disciples not to be like the pagans, who think that by multiplying words they are more likely to be heard; God knows what we need before we ask (Mt 6:7-8). Indeed, anxiety about earthly things implies a lack of faith in God's loving providence (Mt 6:30-32; Lk 12:29-30).

In his version of the "Lord's prayer," Luke presents a model for praying in which petition is placed in its proper context. He begins with the address, "Father" (not "Our Father" [Aramaic *Abinu*] as in Matthew, but simply "Father," corresponding to the *Abba* of Jesus' own prayer): the one to whom we pray is not some omnipotent despot whom we must persuade or placate, but is from the start recognized as the one who has revealed his parental love and care. There follow two expressions of our acceptance of God's lordship: "hallowed be thy name! may thy Kingdom come!" Finally, there are three petitions: for bread; for forgiveness; and for deliverance from the eschatological trial. We should notice that the objects of these petitions are things which the gospel teaches God wishes for us, and which he takes the initiative in providing. There is no question of informing God of our needs, still less of persuading him to be benevolent; these petitions are simply the expansion of what we mean when we accept God's lordship and wish for his kingdom—i.e., the triumph of his love and peace—to come.

This is precisely the key to Christian prayer as petition. It is not a matter of making God amenable to our will—as though we were either wiser or better than he—but of placing ourselves in God's "will," which is love. Persistence in prayer is not for the sake of wearing God down until he gives in, but for the sake of remaining faithful to our confident expectation of his care. (Note that we miss the point of the parable in today's gospel if we treat it as an allegory, in which God corresponds to the unwilling friend who must be roused by persistent knocking. The point is rather one of *contrast*, as is evident in the later part of the passage. If even you, evil as you are, can do good for those you love, how much more will God do so; if even humans can be persuaded by persistent asking to meet others' needs, how much more can we expect our needs to be met by God, who does not need to be persuaded!)

Luke, therefore, tells us that prayer is *always* answered; God always gives to those who ask. But what does he give? Not simply "good things" (cf. Mt 7:11); for Luke, God infallibly gives *his Spirit* to those who ask. But God's "Spirit" is God's way of thinking and being; it transforms us in accord with God's life and values.

This is not to say that we ultimately return to prayer as simple submission to God's "will" in a fatalistic sense. For the "will" of God is not a blueprint or a plan. However much we may depend upon anthropomorphisms in our language and images, we must always finally recall that God is not a finite being, with a finite "mind" and freedom that can change from moment to moment and must strive for a perfection outside themselves. God *is* his will, and God is love. But what the love of God is to be—what it *can* be—in our world is largely up to us. It is we who create the conditions in which God's love can be received; in a sense, one might even say that we create God's "will" by creating the concrete possibilities of love.

Ultimately, then, the prayer of petition is not so much a matter of looking for a response out of the heavens, transforming the world by an extrinsic and almighty power. Rather, it is a matter of making ourselves—like Jesus—the means of God's transformation of the world in his Spirit, the spirit of love. The transformation and power that we look for in prayer are something of which we are a part; something that must first of all transform us. Real prayer is thus the expression in concrete terms of our hope for the triumph of that transformation: the expression also of our willingness to be involved, to be used in bringing about the victory of God's love in our own lives and the lives of one another.

Eighteenth Sunday of the Year

Eccl 1:2; 2:21–23
Ps 95:1–2, 6–7, 8–9
Col 3:1–5, 9–11
Lk 12:13–21

Several years ago a film appeared based on the best-selling novel, *Less Than Zero*. It is the story of a group of college-aged kids who apparently have everything they could desire: money, palatial homes, leisure, and virtually unlimited access to all kinds of pleasure: sex, drugs, liquor. At one point in the story, the following dialogue takes place between two of the main characters:

"You have everything."
"No, I don't."
". . . What don't you have?"
"I don't have anything to lose."

That is, the character realizes that he doesn't have anything whose loss would be felt; he has many things, but nothing worth having. It is the whole point of the story: he and his friends really have "less than zero." They live in a constant whirl of frenetic pleasure-seeking which barely covers over their fundamental unhappiness, shallowness, boredom, and despair.

If the "moral" of the story is that material prosperity does not bring happiness or meaningfulness to life, there is the consolation that at least these spoiled children have the opportunity to realize it early.

There are probably many middle-aged people in our society whose story is the opposite of that of the spoiled children in *Less Than Zero*. Such people grew up with high ideals and a sense of meaning, with a morality of self-sacrifice and a vision of a better world, and at some point were disillusioned. (The immediate cause may have been Vietnam, or the assassination of John F. Kennedy, or the shooting of unarmed students at Kent State, or Watergate; or it may have been simply the wearing pressure of time, of aging, of the constant bombardments of a materialistic and cynical society.) They found their past faith suddenly shattered or slowly eroded; the meanings, values, hopes, became unreal, or impossible, or empty, or too demanding; they turned to material goals and compromised. Yet the thirst remains for something more. As Stanislas Joyce said of his brother James, "When one has once been in love with God in one's youth, it is impossible ever to be satisfied with anything less."

For many such people, it is only the prospect of death (as in today's gospel story) that dissipates the illusion of attaining happiness through material goods or pleasures. And that prospect becomes at some point real for each of us.

But the problem is that the perspective of death—once we take it with absolute seriousness—seems to relativize *all* earthly values. Our first reading, from the book of Qoheleth (Ecclesiastes), speaks of the vanity of laboring for wealth that must be left behind at death; but Qoheleth goes far beyond what we hear in this passage. It is not only material things that are seen as "vanity" in the light of human mortality; wisdom, knowledge, virtue, love are equally "vain," since all end in death.*

Qoheleth's point is made dramatically in Woody Allen's film, *Hannah and Her Sisters*. Mickey, the hero, fears that he

---

* See, for example, Eccl 1:16–18; 6:8–9; 9:1.

has cancer. When he finds that he does not, he is euphoric. But suddenly he realizes that he has only received a momentary reprieve; he will have to die someday. He goes into depression: how can anything in life have meaning or value in the light of the knowledge that we must die and lose everything?

The promise of "eternal life" is of course the central Christian response to human anxiety over the threat of death. But it must be made clear that "eternal life" is not to be understood simply as "life after death"—leaving *this* life essentially valueless. The Christian message proclaims that there is a way of *living* that transcends the vanity and impermanence of the world. One can live in a way that has a permanent value: "Set your heart on what pertains to higher realms," says St. Paul. "Be intent on things above rather than on things of earth" (second reading). This is not to be taken as a simple "otherworldliness"; it is not merely a matter of awaiting our "real" life after death: the new life is *now*, even if its glory is "hidden." Already in this world we can be "rich in the sight of God" (gospel)—that is, "possess" the world and life in a way that goes beyond the reach of death.

The New Testament thus leads us not only beyond the total pessimism of Qoheleth, but also beyond the pessimism about this world enshrined in the platonic myth of the "immortal soul": a spiritual entity which belongs in another world and is temporarily imprisoned in a fleshly form which it must escape in order to be happy. Christian anthropology is more radical. "Eternal life"—the sharing in an ultimate value and way of being—is what we are, in our deepest selves, now, if we are living on the level of what we profess to believe.

The "if" is crucial. Just as the hope of "eternity" is only credible to those whose lives are open to an ultimate self-transcendence, so also with the present value of life. The "evidence" for the worthwhileness of life cannot be found in some "objective" manner; it must be found within, in our experience. But we can only find it in our experience if there *is* such an experience in us; and there can only be such an experience if we choose to live—to take the risk of living—in a transcendent way, in accord with our deepest desires: the desire for love, for "spirit," which is the dimension of being which takes us beyond self to communion with every other and with God.

Nineteenth Sunday of the Year

Wis 18:6–9
Ps 33:1, 12, 18–19, 20–22
Heb 11:1–2, 8–19
Lk 12:32–48

Is there a constitutional right for citizens to have and use firearms? If one listens to the advertisements of the NRA, it is obvious that there is. If, on the other hand, one attends to the arguments of constitutional lawyers, the matter becomes more complex. The constitutional provision concerning bearing arms was written to apply to a civilian militia, and it is not at all clear that it can be taken out of that context, or how it applies to the contemporary situation.

This issue illustrates a more general and simple point: it is very difficult to apply norms from the past to the present. One must ask what is universally applicable, and thus relevant to us, and what belonged to the specific context of the times of origin of this norm, a way of thinking which may now be totally outdated. On the other hand, how does one apply the founders' insights to situations that did not exist in their times? Such questions—which are involved not only in issues like gun control, but also the right of privacy, abortion, capital punishment, etc.—keep the U.S. Supreme Court constantly busy, and give it a power probably unforeseen by its creators.

If such difficulties arise with the meanings and relevance of a precise document like the Constitution, written only 200 years ago, we may assume *a fortiori* that they will be present in our dealings with the gospels, the "good news" about the message and life of a man whose context is removed from us by two millennia.

Christians, of course, take Jesus and his message to be God's revelation, and hence the norm for our belief. But obviously not everything about Jesus is relevant to us on the same level. Jesus was a man of his times, living a particular life in distinctive circumstances. It is clear that at least some of his deeds and words were addressed to the immediate situations he confronted; we cannot presume that everything Jesus said or did was meant to have (or can have) universal validity for all time. (So, for example, we could hardly take Jesus' instructions to his disciples for their preaching mission as guidelines for missionaries today; indeed, we find that the recognition of the need to change them with new circumstances occurs already within the New Testament.)*

In some matters, the limitation of Jesus' words by his context is patent and unproblematic except to the most fundamentalist mentality. But a difficulty arises when the matter is something seemingly fundamental to Jesus' message, as is the case in today's gospel, concerned with the coming of God's kingdom; for here we are faced, not with an external limitation in the scope of application, but with an apparent limitation in Jesus' own mind and way of thinking itself.

The thought of many Jews of Jesus' time was shaped by what has come to be called the "apocalyptic" mentality: they expected the imminent coming of the "eschaton" in an earth-shattering crisis of history, a dramatic intervention of God which would end the world as we know it and establish the messianic kingdom.

Jesus apparently shared this expectation. In the synoptic gospels he speaks of a great trial about to occur, which would include death for himself, a radical test for his followers, and

* Compare, for example, Lk 9:3 with Lk 22:35.

a crisis for all of Israel, ending in the triumph of God through the Son of man, the representative of God's people.[†] This anticipation forms the context for the sayings in today's gospel.

Obviously, things did not happen this way. The end of the world and triumphant establishment of God's kingdom (which the early church associated with the triumphant return of the resurrected Jesus himself) did not occur. This does not exclude, of course, that in a "higher" sense—beyond the time-conditioned concepts and images which were the only medium in which it could find expression—Jesus' eschatological anticipation, founded on his interior sense of the Father's presence, was in fact correct. But its fulfillment came about in a way unforeseen by Jesus' human mind or by his disciples. The immediate world-wide crisis did not occur, either in Jesus' lifetime or in his swift return as the Son of man in glory.

Jesus' followers, therefore, eventually had to ask themselves the meaning of his eschatological warnings, and their question is put in the mouth of Peter in today's gospel, a question to Jesus from the church. The reply interprets Jesus' sayings about the end times in the new context experienced by the first generations of Christians. Even though the master does not come soon, and the time of his coming may be long, his followers must still be waiting. Expectation is not to be a momentary tension, soon relieved; it is to be the church's very way of life.

This permanent tension gives to Christianity its peculiar character. The constant awareness of God as our future can translate into an overwhelming sense of duty, an unceasing anxiety about living up to standards (recall Garrison Keillor's caricature of the church of "Our Lady of Perpetual Respon-

---

† See the so-called "Synoptic Apocalypse": Mt 24; Mk 13; Lk 21.

sibility"). But the real meaning of the gospel is not a threat, nor the loss of the present through the oppression of the future. Jesus begins this discourse with the words, "Do not live in fear." We are awaiting the coming of one we love; it is the overflowing of loving expectation that should create our generosity and our morality.

The Christian lives in joyful hope, a mixture of contentment and discontent. We have joy in the present, because it is going toward completion. The future is not the loss of the "now," but the fulfillment of its promise. On the other hand, this means that there is always a necessary and fruitful discontent with the moment, a dynamism to go beyond. We can—without despair—recognize the flaws in ourselves and the world, and take the responsibility for change. Our hope means that this responsibility is based not on law, or commands, or threats, but on love, on the conviction that love is a final, eternal, and coming reality.

Twentieth Sunday of the Year

Jer 38:4–6, 8–10
Ps 40:2, 3, 4, 18
Heb 12:1–4
Lk 12: 49–53

The words of today's gospel no doubt have a very strange sound to us. We tend to think of religion as a principal support of the sacred value of family. We associate Jesus in particular with love and harmony; in every eucharist we recall his promise of peace and celebrate it among ourselves. It clashes with our image of him to hear him speak of setting families against each other and coming not to bring peace, but division.

The text we have heard presents perhaps even more of a shock when we read it in the parallel passage in Matthew (which does not occur in the Sunday readings), where the same thought is expressed, not abstractly, but in more concrete Aramaic imagery: "I have come not to bring peace, but a sword" (Mt 10:34).

The meaning of Jesus' words was perhaps more readily apparent to earlier ages than our own. In her novel, *In the Wilderness,* set in the Middle Ages, Sigrid Undset describes the reaction of her hero when he hears the words of this passage read in Latin: *"non veni pacem mittere, sed gladium"*:

> *Gladium*—Olav had always thought that word sounded so finely. And he saw that it could not be otherwise: when God Himself descended into the world of men and

appeared as a man among men, it had to be, not peace, but a sword. For God could not intend to be as a sorcerer who puts man's will to sleep; he must needs come with a war-cry: for or against Me!

This is indeed the meaning: God's coming to the world means discernment, choice, the exercise of freedom. The message of Jesus is one of love; but love is not always easy, not always approving. Love is demanding; it wishes the best, and therefore it challenges. It demands freedom and response, and therefore it causes division. (Jewish thought imagined that such division, even among families, would characterize the tumult of the period of the eschatological trial before the coming of God's kingdom.)

Jesus himself had to undergo the trial. He speaks of having a baptism to undergo and a fire to kindle: images of suffering and purification. He is eager for their accomplishment; he is "in anguish" until they are fulfilled. For him, the faithful response to God's love in the world meant division from his own family and nation, and finally betrayal by a friend, passion and death.

The early church also faced a baptism of fire: the trial of persecution. Early Christians had to decide, take a stand for their faith, frequently, like Jesus, in opposition to those closest to them as well as to their society as a whole.

For most of us, the situation is not so dramatic: we are not a persecuted church; for most of us, our faith is a uniting and not a dividing factor in our family life. Yet there is for us—as for other earlier generations of Christians—another kind of trial. The author of the letter to the Hebrews (second reading) exhorts the community to patience and endurance: "Do not grow despondent; do not abandon the struggle." We are perhaps not called to life and death decisions for the faith;

but it also takes courage and discernment to live daily the many small decisions that separate us from the values of the world—or should do so.

The danger to our faith is not apostasy, but erosion. In almost unnoticed ways, we are apt to lose the vision, to forget our motivation, to be swept along with the crowd. We are tempted to forgo our freedom, to renounce using our minds to discern. Our religion itself may become a comfortable escape from the real choice for or against God.

To such of us, the author of Hebrews gives the advice: "Let us keep our eyes fixed on Jesus, who inspires and perfects our faith"; and he reminds us that "we are surrounded by a cloud of witnesses."

Our celebration of the eucharist is for precisely these two things. We remember Jesus, and with him the suffering of the world; and we recognize our communion in the good: we are not alone, but are part of a community quietly deciding to live for the goal of God's love, whatever the cost.

Twenty-First Sunday of the Year

Is 66:18–21
Ps 117:1–2
Heb 12:5–7, 11–13
Lk 13:22–30

A recent op-ed article in *The New York Times* commented on an often overlooked aspect of the drug crisis:

> Drug-related violence has escalated to the point where innocent victims are shot every week, and not-so-innocent drug dealers and aspiring dealers are killed at a rate of about three a day.
>
> Most of these deaths come early to young men who could have been leaders in the city. But instead of pursuing educational avenues, which take time to produce rewards, they turn to the more profitable and alluring business of dealing drugs.... Obviously, the lure of making fast nontaxable money through the illegal drug trade far outweighs the risk not only of prison but of death.

What attracts many young people to the drug trade, apparently, is not just the idea of success, but of *quick* success; success without waiting, without drudgery, self-discipline, or hard work (although in fact, as might be expected, it does not actually happen that way).

In short, people deal drugs for essentially the same reason people start taking drugs: to obtain happiness by a quick fix. A similar mentality seems to stand behind many of the other problems that plague our society: teen-age pregnancies, abortions, the AIDS epidemic. In each of these cases, a major cause of the problem is people's engaging in sexual activity for the sake of pleasure or self-fulfillment or even genuine love, without taking thought of the possible results and assuming responsibility. This in turn seems to be a manifestation of a widespread presumption that one can or should be able to attain happiness or enjoyment without price—not as a "reward" for hard work or as a result of serious commitment, but as a natural right.

In sharp contrast to such an attitude is the spirit of Jesus in today's gospel: "Try to come in through the narrow gate; many will try to enter and will be unable. . . ." This saying does not mean that only a few will be saved. On the contrary, we are told shortly afterwards that people will come from all directions to take their place in the kingdom. Jesus refuses to speculate on the question he is asked—how many will be saved. His point is that those who presume that they are saved—who think themselves the "elect"—are in danger of not entering at all; they will find themselves outside. The way to the kingdom is now open, but the door is "narrow"; one must make an effort to enter. There is no "easy" way. Salvation is not a matter of natural right or of "belonging," whether to the "chosen people" or the church; it requires active striving and struggle.

Why must it be this way? If God loves us, and wishes (as Jesus teaches) to *give* us his kingdom—then why must we work for it? Why must attaining happiness involve labor and even pain?

The letter to the Hebrews (second reading) gives one explanation. Quoting Proverbs (3:11–12), it tells us that "whom the Lord loves, he disciplines." The scriptures appeal to the experience of parenting—"What son is there whom his father does not discipline? At the time it is administered, all discipline seems a cause for grief, not joy; but later it brings forth the fruit of peace and justice to those who are trained in its school. . . ."

On a common sense level, this idea certainly seems true to our experience. We would not consider those children fortunate whose parents simply gave them everything that they desired and shielded them from all pain; on the contrary, we would consider such children to be "spoiled"—in some sense cheated, deprived of an element of their humanity. And this is so because mature personhood involves responsibility, growth, and achievement, and these cannot be attained without a certain denial of the self in order to become something more. Likewise, true happiness is not simply something that you can *get;* it is the result of what you *are,* what you become. It depends upon an inner capacity, and that capacity must be disciplined and developed, for it consists in the ability to go beyond ourselves—to find our real being outside ourselves, in love.

The last point is crucial. The happiness that God wills for us—his "kingdom"—is the deepest possible: the sharing of his own life, the ultimate mystery of love. To attain that love means going beyond the inertia of accepting ourselves as we are and learning to create what we can be; going beyond our spontaneous desires and learning what is truly good; going beyond our spontaneous egotism and learning to find ourselves in others; going beyond mere pleasure and finding genuine happiness. If God truly gives us *himself,* it cannot be otherwise: the mystery of being and love cannot be reduced to what we now are; it must demand that we become a totally new kind of being. There is no shortcut, no quick and easy way to die to self; it must always be the effort to enter through the narrow door.

Twenty-Second Sunday of the Year

Sir 3:17–18, 20, 28–29
Ps 68:4–5, 6–7, 10–11
Heb 12:18–19, 22–24
Lk 14:1, 7–14

One of the great contributions that contemporary psychology has made to theology and to religion in general has been a deeper understanding of the development of the human moral sense. While we may once have thought of conscience in a rather abstract and universal way, it is now clear that there are different kinds and stages of moral apprehension. The psychologist Lawrence Kohlberg, for example, speaks of three major phases of conscience development.

A first stage is characterized by an egocentric point of view. For the very young child, rules and expectations are totally external; they are obeyed because of fear of punishment or expectation of reward or approval. The only motivation for conduct is the effect it will have on one's self. One behaves well toward others in the expectation of receiving good treatment in return.

At a second stage, morality becomes "conventional": the rules of society are internalized; the growing child recognizes a need for order, and sees itself as a part of a society, with which it identifies. The rules now are "our" rules; obedience to them is a part of belonging.

Finally, moral maturity occurs in what Kohlberg calls the "post-conventional" stage. The person makes a free choice of values, and submits to them out of the conviction of their rightness, whether they are in accord with society's norms or not. This is the stage of "conscience" in the proper sense. Values are perceived as real and independent of the self; one may even be called to sacrifice one's self-interest or the approval of others in order to follow what is seen as "right" in itself.

It is obvious that Kohlberg's stages are an idealized systematization of the process of moral maturing. In actual fact, not all people develop in the same way or to the same extent. Some people apparently never get beyond the first stage in their moral lives: they remain egotists. Their overriding concern is for themselves. They are always seeking the first place at the banquet. Their relations with others are based upon using them—even if the price for this is being used in return. These are people who can only understand the profit motive: "What's in it for me? What do I get out of it?"; and they are cynical about any other motivation: "Every man has his price"; no matter what they say, "everyone is really looking out for number one."

Most people, however, develop beyond this perspective in at least some areas of their lives. One would like to think that there are few parents, however egotistical and cynical in their relations with other adults, who do not reach, at least at times, a genuine love for their children: a spontaneous and unselfish generosity, without thought of profit or return; a putting aside, at least momentarily, of the self-centeredness that rules in the rest of life. In some areas, at least, others may have the first place at the banquet.

We can probably presume, in short, that most people have some experience of altruism and of a genuine sense of giving oneself to a value outside the self. But such values and altruism can be quite limited. I may be capable of love of others, but only those others who are in some sense an extension of my selfhood: *my* family, *my* friends, *my* nation. Even love can be an extended egotism. I only invite to the banquet those who can return my hospitality, who in some way reward me.

For Jesus, in contrast, real love must be universal. The attitude we have toward those we care for most deeply should be the basic attitude of life. We should invite to the banquet those who cannot make any return. In doing this, we imitate God, who has invited us to the banquet—of life, or existence—out of sheer generosity, although we can make no return.

It is in this context that we can understand Jesus' counsel that we must humble ourselves.* This has nothing to do with exhibiting a false modesty or self-depreciation. To humble oneself is to recognize and act upon the simple truth of our lowliness before God: the fact that we receive all as gift, and that we are in constant need of his further gift of love or salvation. This realization leads us to have the same attitude of generosity toward others that has been freely manifested to us: to love others open-heartedly and without limit, not for the sake of reward, or because of the need for social order, but because of the infinite value of every humble self which, like our own, is affirmed and loved by God.

* Note that the same saying occurs also in other contexts—see Lk 18:14; Mt 18:4; Mt 23:12.

Twenty-Third Sunday of the Year

Wis 9:13–18
Ps 90:3–4, 5–6, 12–13, 14–17
Philem 9–10, 12–17
Lk 14:25–33

One of the most disconcerting things about learning a foreign language for the first time is making the discovery that a language is not merely a different set of sounds for the same ideas, but embodies a (more or less) different way of perceiving and expressing reality, so that some of one's own common ideas can perhaps not be exactly expressed at all, while common ways of thinking in the new language require a change in one's way of looking at things. In colloquial Chinese, for example, the usual way of asking someone to express a preference is to ask, "Do you like A, or do you like B?" Of course, one may in fact like both; but one expresses one's preference by making a choice between them, and "liking" one or the other.

A somewhat analogous phenomenon occurs in the Aramaic language which was spoken by Jesus and his disciples. Aramaic grammar has no comparative degrees ("I like A more than B; I like C most of all"); to express a dramatic preference, one must resort to contrast ("I *love* A and I *hate* B"). On one level, this linguistic background explains the seemingly harsh words of Jesus in today's gospel, for the Greek text reads, "If anyone comes to me without *hating* [μισεῖ] father and mother," etc., "he cannot be my follower." Of course, this does not mean that the Christian should revile or despise parents or family or self; but it expresses the disproportion between our choice of God, the absolute good, and any other relative good.

79

At the same time, the meaning of this text should not be reduced to a theoretical and abstract "preference" for God. Our translation, which says that the follower of Jesus must "turn his back" on family and self, captures the spirit of the saying in its context: there is a factual cost to "preferring" God; it means the practical willingness to leave all else, however valuable, behind; it means following Jesus to the cross. (It is notable that although the scene of this discourse is set in Galilee, where Jesus' mission has been successful, Luke has told us that he is on his way to Jerusalem: that is, to the culmination of his mission in death.)

The parables which follow emphasize the point. They tell us that we must "count the cost" of discipleship. It is not a matter of deciding whether it is "worthwhile" to come to Jesus, but of recognizing what that option entails: not triumph and ease, but renunciation and conflict. If we are to enter into this life with our eyes open, we need to rethink and reevaluate our relationship with all things and people. Otherwise, we will be unprepared for its demands. Just as we would not build a house or fight a battle without reckoning our resources, just so with the life of faith. Christianity must not be taken for granted.

One can point to many examples of the cost of being a Christian not only in history, but in our contemporary world. One need only think of such figures as Oscar Romero, or the five Jesuit priests slain in El Salvador. For most of us, the conflict with a sinful and unjust world's values and the need to make a choice will probably not be so dramatic. But this in itself is a danger; we can perhaps be lulled into thinking that there is no struggle to be undertaken, no sacrifice demanded, and so make our faith a pretense, a merely mental commitment. The medium in which the total self-surrender is made may vary for each of us; but let us be certain: there can be no Christianity, no following of Jesus, without it.

Twenty-Fourth Sunday of the Year

Ex 32:7–11, 13–14
Ps 51:3–4, 12–13, 17, 19
1 Tim 1:12–17
Lk 15:1–32

In flipping through the channels on the television recently, I caught a few minutes of the beginning of a teen-age comedy film. The premise (from which the rest of the film's plot can easily be guessed) is that a responsible, serious, "uptight" young college student is entrusted with the job of delivering a new car across country. His free-wheeling, lovably manic and girl-crazy roommate and companion encourages him to seize the opportunity to take off for the beaches to have fun. The hero, rejecting the temptation, replies that he simply cannot act so irresponsibly. His final explanation is, "I'm too Catholic."

Catholics have a reputation for taking life seriously; for having an all-pervasive sense of obligation, even guilt (many of us I am sure reacted with a wry sense of recognition to the name Garrison Keillor gave to the local Catholic church in his "Lake Wobegon" stories: "Our Lady of Perpetual Responsibility").

The French existentialist philosopher Jean-Paul Sartre summarized the idea of the God he saw (and rejected) in the Catholic religion in the notion of the "unwatched Watcher": the invisible Judge, always seeing us, holding up to us an impossible ideal of perfection and threatening us with punishment if we fail to attain it. God is the cause of anxiety.

The gospels of the last several Sundays certainly give some understanding of where this kind of idea of God comes from. They present us with a message full of challenges and demands. We are told to enter through the narrow way; to humble ourselves; to take up the cross; to renounce all ties, even to family; to prefer Jesus to everything. And we are warned of the danger of being cast out into the place of weeping and the grinding of teeth. From this perspective on what is expected of us in life, one might anticipate the image of a stern and uncompromising God.

Yet when Jesus speaks of what God is like, it is entirely the opposite. God is a loving parent, who always takes the initiative, who does everything to save. He never ceases to love and to seek out even what is lost; he is like a woman who sweeps out the entire straw floor of her house to find a lost coin, like a shepherd who braves the wilds to search for a single lost sheep, like a loving Father who longs for and seeks out his children even when they reject him.

How can we reconcile this image of an all-loving God with the all-encompassing demands of the gospel?

It is precisely in terms of love—and only so—that the demands make sense. The Christian's responsibility is not a matter of commands imposed from without by a supreme Lawgiver, but the overflowing of love from within. The imperatives of the gospel are simply the demands that we make on ourselves because of what we are; they are the only way to be true to our nature. For the Christian, "responsibility" is undertaken with joy because it truly is a "response" to the experience of being loved absolutely.

It is for this reason that St. Augustine could summarize Christian morality in the single phrase: "Love and do what you will." The perfection of the gospel is what we *desire* if we truly love, truly respond to being loved. If we are like the One who loves us, then we also will wish to sweep out the whole house, go to all lengths in search of what is lost, in joyous imitation of the love with which we have been loved.

Twenty-Fifth Sunday of the Year

Amos 8:4–7
Ps 113:1–2, 4–6, 7–8
1 Tim 2:1–8
Lk 16:1–13

A recent television program on communism in Cuba bore the appropriate title, "The God That Failed." Not only in Cuba, but all over the world it seems that communism as an ideological system, a substitute religion which proposes humanity as its ultimate object of devotion, has failed.

How and why has it failed? Clearly it has failed first of all as an economic and political system: it has failed to provide prosperity for the masses of people. But this failure is due to a deeper one—as a system of belief, it has failed to motivate and convince.

An example may be found in a recent news story. The Soviet government has decided to pay its own farmers in foreign "hard" currency for their grain, in order to persuade them to sell it to the state. The USSR has long grown enough grain to meet all its needs, but in recent years it has nevertheless been a large importer. The reason is that the Soviet farmers preferred to feed their grain to their livestock rather than sell it to the state at the low prices it set. They would make more profit by fattening their animals than by providing food for their fellow citizens. Appeals to patriotism, idealism, comradeship, had no effect; the farmers did not believe in the system enough to sacrifice their own well-being for it.

One might say that communism fails because it neglects self-interest. Theologically, we might say that it disregards the reality that the Christian tradition calls "original sin." It thinks humanity is perfectible, and appeals to idealistic motivations; it has no way of dealing with the factual opportunism of people. Politically it falls prey to evil and power-hungry leaders, and ends in tyranny rather than the freedom it proclaims; socially and economically, it fails to motivate self-seeking individuals, and falls into divisiveness and economic torpor. It appeals to the brother/sisterhood of all people and the high ideal of equality; but it can give no ultimate basis for believing in such ideals or putting them into practice.

Before we gloat over the apparent collapse of Marxism-Leninism as a system of belief, however, we should take a close look at our own society. The Western vision of material progress is also proving to be a "god that failed"; not economically, perhaps (although the evidence is not yet completely in), but spiritually. Consider what we see in our society: rampant addiction to drugs and dependence on alcohol; crime and violence; widespread depression; lack of values and vision; cynicism and vice in politics; the corruption of youth; racial and class conflict; the increasing destitution of the poor; homelessness; the vulgarization of culture; the destruction of the environment and the exploitation of the Third World for profit and the continuance of our "standard of living."

We can see all around us the point that the gospel makes: material goods can become a rival god, one which takes us from the true meaning of life.

There is, of course, a proper meaning and use for material goods. The gospel speaks of using wealth to "make friends" who will provide a "lasting reception" when the world's goods fail. It is not merely a matter of acting cleverly, like the unjust steward, to provide for the future; it is a matter of getting our values straight, distinguishing between ends and means. Persons come first. We should be using our knowledge and wealth for building the human community of love; it is this which is "lasting" in the final analysis, beyond the inevitable loss of all things, even life.

Obviously, we believe this; probably most people in our society would say they believe it. Why is it not more of a reality? Why—as the gospel says—are this world's children so much more energetic and successful than the children of light?

Communism's god of humanity could not overcome self-interest and motivate people to build a new kind of society; can the real God not motivate us either? Is it only the self-interested pursuit of wealth that can be the basis of human social relations? Is the power of "original sin" really greater than grace?

The gospel encourages us to be as energetic in pursuing spiritual values as materialists are in pursuing money. Why not? Imagine what it would be like if the energy used in self-interest could be used for promoting peace, for eliminating hunger, comforting suffering, cleaning up the environment...

It may be that a crisis is needed to inspire us; and such a crisis seems imminent. Scientists are increasingly forceful in their warnings that humanity cannot go on exploiting and polluting the environment as we now are, or we will die as the result of our own technology. But what can be done? Our way of life depends upon this exploitation. The author Bill McKibben in his book, *The End of Nature,* suggests that the impending crisis might provide an unprecedented opportunity:

> If there is one item that virtually all successful politicians on earth—socialist and fascist and capitalist—agree on, it is that "economic growth" is good, necessary, the proper end of organized human activity. Our present environmental troubles, though, just might give us the chance to

change the way we think. What if . . . we began to reject a pervasive individual consumerism, and began to alter a basic way we look at ourselves?

This is the challenge of the gospel: to look at ourselves in a new way, and apply this vision to actual living, to the values we act on. We must reject all the gods that fail—the "mammon" of the gospel—whether communist or capitalist, and seek true wealth in becoming truly human, in valuing the love of others, striving for life in harmony with each other and with the earth that gives us God's gift of life.

Twenty-Sixth Sunday of the Year

Amos 6:1, 4–7
Ps 146:7, 8–9, 9–10
1 Tim 6:11–16
Lk 16:19–31

I can remember that as a young boy I was very disturbed by today's gospel. It was important for me to realize that the parable Jesus tells was only a fictional story, and not "real life." It was not that it inspired in me the fear of damnation; my background made me identify much more with the poor Lazarus, who is saved, than with the rich man who is condemned. I was distressed rather because my tender child's heart could not believe—did not want to believe—that the world was so cold and cruel a place as the parable portrays. I could not accept that any person could really be indifferent to someone starving at his very doorstep.

I never could have imagined that I would actually see the scene portrayed by the gospel with my own eyes—and not in Calcutta or Somalia, but in New York and Washington, in Bay Shore and Huntington, in big cities and little towns throughout the most prosperous nation in the world.

This gospel story today has a frightening actuality, even to its details. "Lazarus longed to eat the scraps that fell from the rich man's table." How many of us have not actually seen people on the city streets foraging through garbage cans, looking for their next meal?

But the relevance of the parable becomes more dramatic when we look beyond what we actually see; for, as bad as the situation may be in our own nation, the real name of Lazarus today (as Pope John Paul II has said) is the Third World. There are twelve of them—the poor—for each of us in the prosperous nations; and because of the technology of the electronic age, they are also immediately outside our door. They have seen us piling up so much garbage that we no longer know how to get rid of it; polluting the air and the water that we all must use; despoiling the natural resources not only of our own land, but of theirs as well, in order to support our life-style.

The ultimate causes of the disparity of wealth are not here the question. The point is not to establish or escape blame for the situation. In the gospel, the rich man is not said to be the *cause* of the poor man's misery; he is condemned, rather, because he is *indifferent* to it (cf. first reading: "Woe to the complacent in Zion!"). The point is human solidarity: we are in this together.

That solidarity is a fact. Our consciousness of it is already at work. The world is not completely cold and heartless. If things are not so bad as they might be for great portions of humanity—ourselves included—it is because the Christian vision of responsibility and love has to some degree taken root, and has changed the world. There are structures of caring in churches, communities, and even governments.

But the vision and the commitment must continually be renewed. It is this, I think, that makes the message so difficult. *Of course* we are not heartless; *of course* we would not let someone starve outside our door. But there are always new Lazaruses appearing; the job is never done. And it is an unpleasant side of life to look at continually; we would rather do our duty, and be at peace.

The message of the eucharist is precisely about that peace. It tells us that we can find it only in communion with the brokenness of the world, symbolized by the brokenness of Jesus, the brokenness of this bread we share. It is the promise and reality of unity from what is broken, life from pain and suffering, when undertaken in love, that give us the courage to face again the hunger and need in ourselves and in the world.

Twenty-Seventh Sunday of the Year

Hab 1:2–3; 2:2–4
Ps 95:1–2, 6–7, 8–9
2 Tim 1:6–8, 13–14
Lk 17:5–10

One of the great devotions of the Muslim religion is the repetition of and meditation on the names of God; that is, on the titles designating his qualities and his actions on the world. As frequently happens in all religions, this beautiful devotion sometimes degenerated in popular understanding into a means of obtaining spiritual power; it was thought that the constant meditation on one of God's attributes would lead to the growth of a corresponding power in the devotee. Thus there is a legend about a certain Osman Baba, who so constantly addressed God by his title "Ya Qahhar" ("O Destroyer"—for God not only creates the world, but will bring it to its end) that he gained the ability to kill people at will by his spiritual power.

It is not difficult for us to recognize in such a story what we would regard as total misunderstanding of faith. The use of God or of religion for one's earthly and ego-centered ends is not faith, but superstition and magic. If we understand faith properly, we realize that it is not a matter of learning some supernatural means of getting our way, but of entering into God's way. The parable of Jesus about the master and slave is a reminder of this; it is God's world. Not only can we not force God's hand, but he cannot be put under any obligation; whatever we may do "for" him, we have done no more than we ought. But God's lordship is not to be understood in a merely extrinsic sense in which God is our "master" because of his power; God is more profoundly the *goal* of our existence, the source of all value; therefore he cannot be treated as a *means* to obtaining some self-centered purpose.

At the same time, the gospel makes it clear that our faith in God *should* in fact be a means of power in the world. Jesus uses Semitic hyperbole to indicate that faith should be able to work wonders, to do what is seemingly impossible. (The uprooting of a sycamore tree—which was thought to have very deep roots—and the planting of it in the sea indicates a double impossibility. Matthew's version of the same idea has become proverbial: faith can "move mountains" [Mt 17:20].) Faith should be powerful, not in gaining our egotistical desires, but in the miracle of changing the world into God's kingdom of love and peace. But where is this power? Is there a rebuke insinuated in Jesus' response to the disciples; "if you *had* faith . . ."?

Let us note that the whole question of faith's power makes little sense if we are thinking of "faith" merely as the intellectual belief that certain things are true. Jesus is not implying that simply holding certain ideas will change the world; nor is faith a species of stubborn wishful thinking. "Faith" in the biblical context indicates a living relation to God—of which intellectual conviction is, of course, a part. That relation includes trust, confidence, acceptance of God's loving will, and a life which expresses these. Faith, therefore, is intimately connected with love. (It is notable that in the apocryphal Gospel of Thomas, the saying about moving mountains is associated with love: "If two make peace with one another in the same house, they will say to this mountain, 'move,' and it will.")

Faith—in its fullest dimension, as a life of love, lived in confident response to God's self-revelation—introduces a new dimension into the world, and makes what would otherwise be impossible, real. It does so not by any magical force, but by raising human existence to a new level: the level of God's life among us, transcending our "natural" horizon of being. It is impossible for stones and clay to feel or perceive or work against the inexorable laws of physics, but what is impossible on a merely physical level becomes normal everyday reality on the level of life. It is impossible for animals to think, to be self-aware, to transcend environment and their instinctive reactions to it, but such wondrous, incredible events from the point of view of mere biology are the very stuff of the human life lived in consciousness, intelligence and freedom. Our technology even makes it literally possible to change the face of the earth and the rules of nature; to grow plants in water and to move mountains.

But our human existence seems bound by other impossibilities: our incapacity to live at peace with ourselves or each other, our inability to overcome the slavery of egotism and competition, our powerlessness in the face of death. But faith is a life on a new level, in which the impossible becomes real, because a new dimension—the dimension of spirit, of the divine life of love—is introduced to the world. In this dimension we can perform the wondrous, the seemingly impossible acts of unselfish love, of forgiveness, of communion, of life freely surrendered in the hope of eternal validity. In faith, we have power that can change the world. But the condition is the same as that with which Jesus challenged his disciples: if we *have* faith. . . .

Twenty-Eighth Sunday of the Year

2 Kgs 5:14–17
Ps 98:1, 2–3, 3–4
2 Tim 2:8–13
Lk 17:11–19

Several years ago, at the height of the violence in El Salvador, that country was struck by a devastating earthquake. On top of crushing poverty, civil war, death squads, terrorism, came natural disaster. It was a striking example of the "unfairness" of human misery. Misfortune is a fact of life, but one would like to think that there is some proportion in it; that it will somehow be "spread out" evenly. One would think that people who have cancer should be immune to toothache or common colds—they already have their share of suffering. But it is not so; there are no limits. Suffering is not "fair"; it follows no rules; there is no "justice" in it.

There is a tendency among many religious people to think that our suffering somehow comes from God, or at least is under his control. The scriptures—particularly certain parts of the Old Testament—give some support to this idea. But in the last analysis, is this not also an attempt to put some kind of meaning into evil—another sign of our unwillingness to admit that we encounter something really and ultimately irrational, absurd?

For Jesus, on the other hand, suffering and evil are not part of God's plan; they are opposed to God and to his rule. It is for this reason that when God encounters the world in Jesus, it must be as healing.

The cures worked by Jesus in the gospels are therefore

not simply arbitrary acts of power or of mercy; they are the intrinsic signs of the presence of God and his kingdom in the world. A loving God in a sinful, suffering and alienated world cannot be other than healing, liberating, saving, on all levels of reality.

The New Testament notion of the "kingdom" or "rule" of God does not simply refer to the establishment of his power, his absolute "will;" it means also concretely what that power brings about, what God's will for the world is: God's peace (*shalom*)—the state of harmony for which he created all things. Thus God's rule inevitably implies the reestablishment of rightness in the world.

The "rightness" is a spiritual reality; a right relation to God and to others. But is has effects on the world; the healing reaches outward, so to speak, even to the physical level. We hear frequently in the gospels that Jesus' healings are the result of faith—a mental attitude of openness to God's love changes the physical world of the believer; the physical healing is the "sign" of the deeper reality of conversion, the inbreaking of God's kingdom.

What we call "miracles"—like the cures in the gospel—are simply the extraordinary and dramatic instances of what is meant to be the entirely normal result of faith: the healing of the world. It will not usually take place "miraculously"—that is, the way it happens will not be hidden. It will usually take place in the normal way that spirit or mind, inspired and empowered by God in faith, changes matter: by attention to problems, sympathy, intelligent planning, discovery, decision, love, collaboration among people. It will mean that the meaninglessness of suffering is given meaning by becoming the occasion for self-transcendence in faith and the call for loving concern.

In the gospel, the final result of faith's breakthrough is not simply healing, but also thanksgiving. The same holds true for us. We gather in thanksgiving for the work of Jesus, and for the continuance of that work through us. The healing of our spirits creates a communion which has already begun to change the world; which brings us to reach out to human suffering wherever it occurs; which makes us capable of dedicating ourselves to the furthering of healing and forgiveness which form the Kingdom of God on earth.

Twenty-Ninth Sunday of the Year

Ex 17:8–13
Ps 121:1–2, 3–4, 5–6, 7–8
2 Tim 3:14 – 4:2
Lk 18:1–8

In the expanded version of Alexander Solzhenitsyn's novel, *August 1914*, there is a scene of a conversation between a middle-aged former revolutionary and two young radicals. The older man has returned to Russia after a long exile, and has accomodated to the status quo; he has decided that capitalism is not so bad after all; the oppression is not so very great. In any case, one can do much more good by working within the system. The young people are outraged; they see this turnabout as a betrayal, a loss of principle and of heart.

For Solzhenitsyn, the situation is more complex. The older man (in the light of the novelist's hindsight) is right—at least in part—while the young people have their hearts in the right place, but are naive.

At the same time, there is a human dimension to the conversation which transcends its particular historical circumstances. It points, in fact, to a virtually universal phenomenon. As we get older, we become more mellow, less eager for change, even when it may be called for; we lower our expectations of what is possible in life; we practice "realism"—which sometimes means that we lose our high ideals.

Clearly, there is a wisdom that comes with age, but there is also a danger: the danger of narrowing our horizons, losing our vision, of accepting things too easily, of making compromises of principle because we no longer have expectations of life, or because we no longer have the courage to take risks.

There is the danger of disillusionment and cowardice, giving up on life's possibilities and clinging desperately to what we now have and see too quickly passing away.

By contrast, Christianity is about hope. It presupposes an orientation to the future, and demands that we live in expectation.

This is the message of our gospel parable: do not lose heart. The point is not, keep praying always, because you must convince God, but rather, do not give up—continue to trust and expect, even though the answer is not apparent.

Jesus is telling his disciples that in *contrast* with the unjust judge—who only reluctantly performs his duty of caring for the widow—God eagerly strives for his love to take effect.

But the realization of God's love depends upon us; this is the relevance of the mysterious phrase at the end of today's reading: "When the Son of Man comes, will he find any faith on earth?"

In the gospel's view, the question is not, "Will God answer my prayers?," but "Are you ready for God's answer? Are you ready, waiting faithfully for the love of God to transform you and the world, to make you his instrument in the transformation?" This is the significance of "praying always": not losing heart, but living in anticipation.

The lack of expectations and hope becomes a self-fulfilling prophecy. God works through humanity, and thus through our faith, our trust, our belief in his ability to change us and the world, and our willingness to face that change.

In this sense, Christianity is a young religion and religion of the spiritually young; a religion of those who do not lose heart. And it is hope and expectation—a hope that the wisdom of age realizes can only finally be from God and in God—that keep us young. As St. Paul says: "Though my outer being is wasting away, my inner being is renewed from day to day" (2 Cor 4:16).

Thirtieth Sunday of the Year

Sir 35: 12–14, 16–18
Ps 34:2–3, 17–18, 19, 23
2 Tim 4:6–8, 16–18
Lk 18:9–14

Many of those who were alive and thinking during the sixties will probably recall a song recorded by the folk singer Joan Baez entitled, "There but for Fortune." The verses catalogue a number of outcasts of society, and at the end of each comes the refrain, "There but for fortune, go you or I."

A more theological version of the thought was attributed to Cardinal Newman. Coming upon a derelict on the street, he is supposed to have said, "There but for the grace of God goes John Henry Cardinal Newman." Similar sayings have been attributed to John Bunyan and John Wesley. The quote apparently originated, however, with the sixteenth-century English Protestant preacher John Bradford, who remarked, on seeing a group of criminals being led to execution, "But for the grace of God, there goes John Bradford." (Bradford was, in fact, later burned at the stake in the religious persecutions under the reign of Mary Tudor.)

We would probably take Bradford's or Newman's statement as a sign of humility. But if so, exactly how does it differ from the unacceptable prayer of the Pharisee in today's gospel, which Jesus presents as a sign of self-righteousness? Note that the Pharisee does not merely recount the virtues which set him apart from others; he *thanks* God for them. (The Pharisee's prayer, in fact, bears a similarity to a blessing recited by men which perdures even to modern times in the Jewish prayer book: "Blessed art Thou, O Lord our God, King of the Universe, who hast not made me a Gentile . . . a slave . . . a woman. . . .") The Pharisee sees his righteousness as the sign of God's favor. How does this differ from saying, "There but for the grace of God go I?"

It is not a matter of the Pharisee's having a distorted or biased sense of values (as we might think in regard to the prayer quoted above, thanking God for not being a woman); the virtues he thanks God for are real virtues; the qualities he is glad not to have are real vices. The tax collector with whom he compares himself is a real and public sinner—it was in the nature of the job to be a collaborator with the Roman occupiers and an extortionist besides.

What is wrong with the Pharisee's attitude is that he sees God's blessing as setting him apart from others, rather than creating solidarity with them. Externally he thanks God; but his thanks are really a way of exalting himself, since he thinks that God's gifts show that God loves and favors him and *not* the others. Thus Luke characterizes the parable as being addressed to "those who believed in themselves as being righteous, while holding everyone else in contempt." Jesus' message, by contrast, (especially as presented by Luke) is that God's love is universal: not only extensively—God loves all people—but also intensively—God never ceases loving; he loves the sinner, no matter how apparently lost.

In contrast to the Pharisee, the tax collector does the one necessary thing: he faces the painful truth about himself. He admits (truthfully) that he is a sinner, that he has no claim upon God; but he looks for and expects God's mercy. It is this attitude of complete dependence upon God, the recognition of one's own utter poverty, which is true humility.

This attitude leads not to separation from others, but to

solidarity; not merely to the insight, "there but for the grace of God go I," but to the further recognition: there goes one whom God loves as he loves me; and hence, one whom I—who have received all I have as his free gift—must love as I love myself.

Thirty-First Sunday of the Year

Wis 11:22 – 12:1
Ps 145:1–2, 8–9, 10–11, 13, 14
2 Thess 1:11 – 2:2
Lk 19:1–10

Insight into the absoluteness or ultimacy of God—the fact that God alone is God, that he is unique, that he alone is what cannot not be and that all depends upon him for its very being—is the heart of the philosophical and religious conception of God that characterizes classical Western theism. It is the essence of what is meant by the "omnipotence" of God, and it is a conception which is common to all the great Western religions.

Yet within that conception there can be very different notions of what God's absoluteness implies for us. If we truly realize what the word "God" means, and truly believe in his reality, must we not tremble in fear before the inconceivable divine majesty? Are we not reduced to nothingness before the One for whom "the whole universe is as a grain . . . or a drop of morning dew" (first reading)? Is the ultimate religious attitude one of submission to an all-powerful and unquestionable Will? And when we fail to submit to that Will—what consequence can befall us, if not ultimate tragedy?

It is in this context that we hear as truly "good news" the message of God's acceptance of sinners proclaimed by Jesus.

Jesus' treatment of Zacchaeus embodies this message in dramatic terms. It is also a concrete example of the problem caused by it. The gospels advert several times to the fact that

101

Jesus' willfully associating and eating with sinners—that is, his admission of openly and notoriously sinful people to his company and fellowship*—causes scandal for the pious Pharisees. It is taken for granted that Zacchaeus, as a tax-farmer, is a truly wicked person: one who has become wealthy by fraud and extortion, a collaborator with the occupying Roman government, a traitor to and persecutor of his own people. There is, of course, no question of Jesus' approving such conduct; but by entering into the sacred fellowship of a meal with such a person, Jesus implicitly claims the right to admit him—despite his sins—to the fellowship with God which Jesus claimed to proclaim and represent.

One can understand the scandal of pious Jews; it all seems very unfair, even immoral. Can Jesus really be speaking for God when he implies that a lifetime of evil is forgiven, just like that? What of God's justice? Will not the all-powerful God punish sin?

It is in the light of the creative love of God, proclaimed already in the prophets and the Wisdom writings, that we must understand Jesus' message of forgiveness. God is much better than we expect—or fear. Inconceivable as it might seem, the all-powerful, transcendent being actually cares for, loves, his creatures. Indeed, it is precisely because God is the all-powerful creator that he is forgiving:

> . . . you have mercy upon all, because you can
> do all things;
>   and you overlook the sins of men that
> they may repent.
>   For you love all things that are,
> and loathe nothing that you have made.
> (First reading)

* See, for example, Mk 2:13–17, Lk 5:27–32; Mt 9:9–13; also Mt 26:6–13, Mk 14:3–9, Lk 7:36–50.

Compare this message of forgiveness with the Almighty's reaction to sin in the *Qur'an,* where God reveals to Muhammad:

> If We had so willed, we could have given every soul its guidance; but the word from Me concerning evil-doers took effect: that I will fill hell with the jinn and humankind together.[†]

For the Judeo-Christian tradition, God's love and forgiveness are at one with his very act of creating, the essentially loving act of bringing into being what need not be. Furthermore, the act of forgiveness is itself creative. Zacchaeus does not remain a sinner, but is converted; he makes restitution beyond what is required by the Law,[‡] and is filled with compassion for others ("I give half my income to the poor").

What has this to say to us? Certainly it is necessary to hear again and again the message of God's love and forgiveness. It is also necessary for us to ask ourselves not only whether we accept and believe it, but whether we show it and make it known to others. The wonder of this transcendent love is easily forgotten by humans who remake God in their own image. Zacchaeus belonged to the religious tradition that our first reading comes from; so did the Pharisees. But neither recognized or found the forgiveness implied in that tra-

---

[†] Surah XXXII, 13. It should be noted that this is not Islam's only perspective on God, who is also called "the Beneficent, the Merciful." We should also keep in mind that one can find passages in the Judeo-Christian scriptures and tradition which speak of a vengeful and arbitrary God. But it is true that mainstream Islam on the whole tends to emphasize God's all-encompassing power, even to the point of a theology of predestination.

[‡] Lev 6:5; Num 5:7; cf. Ex 22:1, 4, 7.

dition. It required Jesus' surprising (and to some scandalous) intervention to bring it forth. Our religion as well proclaims the God of love and forgiveness. Is that message embodied in a way that sinners—ourselves included—can hear and believe it?

2 Mac 7:1–2, 9–14
Ps 17:1, 5–6, 8, 15
2 Thess 2:16 – 3:5
Lk 20:27–38

The idea of a religion with no promise of an afterlife would no doubt strike most of us as very strange. Indeed, for many people the hope and terror of life after death are the central reason for religious belief. The philosopher Kant saw the idea of immortality, with just reward and punishment, as the necessary condition for the rationality of moral behavior; Shakespeare's Hamlet sees in it the motive for bearing with life itself:

> For in that sleep of death what dreams may come
> When we have shuffled off this mortal coil,
> Must give us pause. . . .
> . . . . who would fardels bear,
> To grunt and sweat under a weary life,
> But that the dread of something after death,
> The undiscover'd country from whose bourn
> No traveller returns, puzzles the will,
> And makes us rather bear those ills we have
> than fly to others that we know not of?
> (*Hamlet,* Act III, scene 1)

Yet we must recall that large portions of humanity—not least our own spiritual ancestors, the ancient Jews—have lived, frequently morally and religiously, with little or no concept of an afterlife. Until only a few centuries before the birth

of Christ, the notions of an "immortal soul" and of the "resurrection of the dead" were alien to Hebrew thought. Even at
the time of Jesus, as today's gospel reminds us, one of the
major Jewish sects, the Sadducees, rejected such ideas (which
both they and their Pharisaic opponents who accepted them
seem frequently to have conceived rather naively in terms of
a heavenly prolongation of earthly life). For the Sadducees,
these notions were innovations of the Hellenistic world; they
preferred to hold to the old religion centered on relation with
God in this world alone.

If the religion of the Sadducees seems foreign to us, the
same cannot be said of their incredulity with regard to eternal
life. However strong may be our own faith and hope, it cannot be denied that a great many modern people—among
them some who believe strongly in God and a morality of
love (like Miguel de Unamuno's saintly priest in his story,
San Manuel Bueno, Mártir) find the idea of survival beyond
death totally unbelievable. Unamuno himself, in his philosophical masterpiece, *Del Sentimiento Tragico de la Vida* (*The
Tragic Sense of Life*), concludes that we must live *as though*
there were an eternal life; but he nevertheless finds such a
belief thoroughly irrational: "Individual human consciousness depends upon the organization of the body . . . everything leads us to conjecture rationally that death implies the
loss of consciousness. Just as before birth we did not exist,
and have absolutely no personal recollection of that time, so
after death we will not be. That is what reason tells us."

Jesus' reply to the Sadducees' objections against the resurrection follows the pattern of rabbinic argumentation. God
is the God of the living, not the dead (see, v.g., Ps 88:11–13).
Being "God of" someone implies a reciprocal relation, and
hence life. But God describes himself to Moses as the God of
Abraham, Isaac, and Jacob (Ex 3:6), who had all died long
before; hence they must be "resurrected" or eternally alive

with God (note that in this context "resurrection" is simply
the symbolic way of speaking of life after death, without necessarily implying a literal raising of the earthly body).

While Jesus' argument apparently impressed his audience (v. 39), the appeal to a literal interpretation of a biblical
text will hardly persuade most modern people who are as-
sailed by doubt. Nor do the classical arguments for the immortality of the soul help greatly in the modern context.
Whatever may be their intrinsic validity, the abstract met-
aphysical notions of "substance" and "immateriality" on
which they are based find little resonance in contemporary
consciousness.

We find quite another approach—one which is perhaps
ultimately more in accord with the spirit of the gospel—in a
dialogue in Fyodor Dostoyevski's great novel, *The Brothers
Karamazov*. A well-to-do woman has come for counsel from
the wise monk, Father Zosima. She cries:

> "I am suffering! Forgive me! I am suffering!"
> "You are suffering? From what are you suffering?"
> "I suffer . . . from lack of faith."
> "Lack of faith in God?"
> "Oh, no, no! I dare not even think of that. But life
> after death—it is such an enigma! And no one, no one
> can solve it . . . The thought of life beyond the grave fills
> me with anguish, with terror . . . I say to myself, 'What if
> I've been believing all my life, and when I come to die
> there's nothing but weeds growing on my grave?'. . . .
> How—how can I get back my faith? I only believed when
> I was a little child, mechanically, without thinking of any-
> thing. How, how is one to prove it? . . . How can I con-
> vince myself? It's deadly, deadly!"
> "No doubt. But there's no proving it, though you
> can be convinced of it."
> "How?"

"By the experience of active love. Strive to love your neighbor actively and constantly. In so far as you advance in love you will grow surer of the reality of God and of the immortality of your soul. If you attain perfect self-forgetfulness in the love of your neighbor, then you will believe without doubt. Doubt will no longer be able to enter your soul. This has been tried. This is certain."

In order to believe in eternal life, we must have the experience of that which eternal life consists of—love. Only by *living* eternal life, the life of love, can we believe—indeed, know—that it is real. Only if we already have in ourselves the life of resurrection, a life whose meaning goes beyond any earthly motivation or explanation, can we feel in ourselves the life which overcomes death. For ultimately what we hope for is not simply a "new" life when this one is over, but the manifestation in its eternal validity of what we are already now, in our profoundest depths: spirit which is immortal because it is the sharing of the very spirit of God, who is love.

Thirty-Third Sunday of the Year

Mal 3:19–20
Ps 98:5–6, 7–8, 9
2 Thess 3:7–12
Lk 21:5–19

It is surely significant of the times we live in that virtually all the events prophesied in Luke's dual apocalyptic vision (the crisis of the fall of Jerusalem and that of the final coming of Jesus) could be correlated with the headlines of the newspapers of the last month—or almost any month one might choose.

"Wars and insurrections": war and revolution in Cambodia, Nicaragua, Mozambique, Northern Ireland, the Middle East. . . .

"Earthquakes, plagues and famines": earthquake in California; the plague of AIDS; drought and starvation in central Africa. . . .

"In the sky fearful omens": a great hole observed in the ozone layer, threatening drastic climatic changes; a tornado in New York leaves seven children dead. . . .

"They will manhandle and persecute you": six Jesuit priests barbarously murdered at a university in El Salvador. . . .

We are not likely, however, to see any of these things either individually or in conjunction as visitations from God or as signs of his coming. On the contrary, we spontaneously regard our history as radically secular: devoid of divine intervention or supernatural significance. The events around us are signs neither of God's anger nor his pleasure; the daily tragedies of life, on the personal and global levels, signify nothing but our vulnerability to our own failures, our awesome responsibility for our own fate.

Even calamities of nature now bear the stamp of humankind. An earthquake may be due to long-standing geological factors beyond our ken and control; but the highway whose collapse caused the death of so many people in the California quake of 1989 was built by human beings. Indeed, such is the impact of human life on the intricate interplay of forces on our planet that we begin to wonder whether any earthly event can be seen as purely "natural." Was it "nature" that caused the tornado that broke down a school wall in New York this week, killing seven children, or was it the "Greenhouse effect" of human pollution of the atmosphere which is radically changing our climate? It becomes harder and harder to distinguish.

The same secular attitude holds true with regard to the positive events of history. When the amazing events of the dissolution of Communist power in Eastern Europe and its liberalization began to take place, very few people, I think, regarded them as the direct result of all those "Hail Mary's" we used to say after Mass for the conversion of Russia. They are seen, rather, as the consequence of inner-worldly factors of economics and politics and the personal charism of particular leaders.

By the same token, the "blessings" in our individual lives are seen less as the result of God's beneficence than of our own work, in conjunction with the opportunities offered by our social situation. Our feast of Thanksgiving, for example, has become a major celebration of both family and nation; we gather together and rejoice in our connections and in our material fortune. But how many people truly feel grateful to God for what they celebrate? How many genuinely think that the food on the table or the money that bought it or the

economic and political system that made the earning possible
are *his* gifts? Is not the connection of God with the feast for
most people a mere ceremonial appendage, a nostalgic rem-
nant of a more mythological mind-set from the past?

There are, of course, those who reject the secularity of
the world; who would like to see life as a continual and direct
dialogue with the all-powerful, all-controlling God, intervening to shape history and personal life. Such a vision is
appealing to many; it gives a certain comfort and security; it
diminishes the heavy burden of responsibility that we bear.
But for most of us, a return to a naive supernaturalism is
impossible. But this does not mean that God is irrelevant,
that there is no meaning to thanksgiving, to expectation,
prayer, or salvation from God. Human history and human
life are ours to make; yet they *are* the sign of God: not a God
intervening from above, but always and everywhere already
present, *in* the world, acting in and through human agents,
human intelligence, human love. God is within; God is the
dynamism of hope and creativity, calling us beyond, making
possible a future and an eternity. The triumphs of history are
the triumph of God's love, working silently, secretly, name-
lessly in us. Its calamities are the failures of love, but at the
same time the call to renewal and hope: "by patient endurance you will save your lives."

Thirty-Fourth Sunday of the Year: Feast of Christ the King

2 Sam 5:1–3
Ps 122:1–2, 3–4, 4–5
Col 1:12–20
Lk 23:35–43

The modern world is certainly not lacking in examples of power; power on a level unimaginable in former ages. Even as political forms have evolved toward democracy, the concrete authority wielded by heads of state, involving as it does decisions that can literally affect the fate of the entire world, has grown more extreme. In many ways the power of an elected American President—to say nothing of a Soviet party chief or the head of a terrorist organization—far exceeds the power of any king of the past.

In the context of our experience of this kind of power, the celebration of the feast of Christ "the King" as an expression of the power of Christ can not only appear to be anachronistic, but even to have a certain element of unreality or even fantasy about it. It is true, of course, that the message of Christ has played an enormous role in the development of Western civilization. But the larger part of the world still remains ignorant of or indifferent to the message and the person of Jesus. Even those countries which could once be qualified as "Christian" are now concretely dominated by influences which have little to do with Jesus or his proclamation. What kind of power does this "King" have?

Certainly we would be entirely missing the significance

112

of this feast if we thought in terms of either the triumphalism and splendor once associated with royalty, or the ability to demand or coerce obedience. Today's gospel presents to us the crucified Jesus: a figure of desolation, powerlessness, disillusionment and apparent failure. The title above the cross, "the King of the Jews," is the height of irony. How can this man have power for us, power to save, if he has not the power to save himself?

It is, of course, only in the light of the resurrection that we can see the true significance of the "Kingship" of Christ. But the resurrection does not undo the cross; it does not suddenly introduce exactly the triumphant "rule" of power which Jesus in his life had renounced. The power of Christ remains that of love, not of coercion; transformation, not conquest. To call Christ "King" is nothing other than to affirm *this* power of his resurrection—i.e., of his becoming the source of life *through* his submission to death. As St. Paul says, he is "the first born of the dead, *so that* primacy may be his in everything." (Second reading).

It must be acknowledged that a spirituality of the cross has sometimes been used in the past to sustain an ideology of submission and passivity in the face of social injustices. Such ideas are a betrayal of the prophetic gospel dynamism to love and justice. On the other hand, the "Kingship" of Christ cannot be used as the legitimation of the exercise of coercive power, either temporal or spiritual, whether by the "left" or the "right." To use Jesus in this way is to empty the cross of its meaning; it is to say that Jesus must come down from the cross, if he is truly King (cf. Mk 15:32, Mt 27:42).

This means that the power of God—the "Kingdom" of God and of his Christ—is something very different from the power of the world and its rulers, be they tyrants or democratically elected officials. It is not a power that saves us from the trials and sufferings of life by an intervention from heaven, like an invasion of the Marines. It is rather the power that overcomes evil by generosity and commitment, even to the point of suffering and death; it is the power of hope to transform the world and its structures from within by the vision of self-giving love.